KNITS FROM THE GREENHOUSE

Published by Interweave Books, an imprint of F+W Media, Inc., 10151 Carver Road, Suite 300, Blue Ash, Ohio 45242. First Edition.

fwcommunity.com

Interweave®

interweave.com

23 22 21 20 19   5 4 3 2 1

SRN: 19KN05

ISBN-13: 978-1-63250-690-0

Editorial Director Kerry Bogert

Editor Jodi Butler

Technical Editor Tian Connaughton

Art Director & Cover Designer
Ashlee Wadeson

Interior Design pnormandesigns

Illustrator Ann Swanson

Photographer
Harper Point Photography

Hair & Makeup Valerie Salls

Photo Stylist Tina Gill

Production Coordinator
Debbie Thomas

contents

common
sanfoin

BATHING BEACH AND BOARD WALK, ONTARIO BEACH PARK, ROCHESTER, N. Y.

INTRODUCTION

Dear Friend,

Winter has finally broken and the smell of lilacs is heavy in the air. I find myself eager to cast on something special for the seasons ahead. Imagining the need for warm-weather friendly wears, I've been on the hunt for the best projects to enhance yarns spun and blended with plant-based fibers—cotton, linen, flax, hemp, and others. Perhaps you've been searching too?

As you know, these fibers are unique. Each has distinctive properties to be considered and celebrated: Cotton tends to grow over time; linen becomes buttery soft with wear; silk has such beautiful drape. There is so much potential for creation!

In these pages you'll find a collection of patterns designed to feature the very best qualities of these fibers. I like to think of them as a hand-picked gathering of blooms from an illusory greenhouse of yarn. I hope you enjoy them as much as I do.

Yours in knitting,
Cornelia

dappled
leaves

pinnate

puget

ACCESSORIES

shawl : wrap : totes : stole : scarf

parterre

spring sprout

stonecrop

GOSSYPIUM ARBOREUM

dappled leaves scarf

Earthy and sophisticated with just a touch of whimsy, this charming accessory adds elegance to any outfit. Worked in a longer length, the scarf can be worn fully extended for a dramatic effect or wrapped around the neck to show off the pretty leafy points.

BY MICHELE PELLETIER

finished size
About 112" × 13" (284.5 × 33 cm) after blocking.

yarn
Fingering weight (#1 super fine).

Shown here: Shibui Knits Reed
(100% linen/flax; 246 yd [225 m]/
1¾ oz [50 g]): 2041 Pollen, 3 skeins.

needles
Size U.S. 4 (3.5 mm).

*Adjust needle size if necessary to
obtain the correct gauge.*

notions
Scrap yarn or extra interchangeable needle cord for
provisional cast-on; 4 stitch markers to separate
stitch pattern sections if wanted; tapestry needle.

gauge
25.5 sts and 24.5 rows = 4" (10 cm) in
leaf edge stitch pattern on size U.S. 4
(3.5 mm) needles after blocking.

notes
— If working from charts, please note that Dappled
Leaves Body chart and Dappled Leaves Decrease
chart A do not include the garter stitch border.
For the border, you will need to knit three stitches
before beginning the chart and after working the
chart on every round. WS rows are not charted
and will be worked: K3, purl to last 3 sts, k3.

— After completing the first half of the scarf,
you will join your yarn on the wrong side and will
work one WS row: K3, purl to last 3 sts, k3.

— Knitting begins with a provisional cast-on.
Work the first half until it is 9" shorter
than desired, then begin decreasing. The
second half begins by attaching the yarn on
the wrong side and working a WS row before
beginning to work the pattern again.

stitch guide

CDD
Slip 2 stitches together knitwise, knit the
next stitch on the left needle, pass the 2
slipped stitches over the knit stitch.

Body

Using a provisional cast-on, CO 69 sts onto scrap yarn or a spare interchangeable cable.

Begin working from Dappled Leaves Body chart or written instructions.

BEGIN DAPPLED LEAVES BODY CHART

The garter borders are not shown on the chart. For the border, knit three stitches before starting each row of the chart pattern, and knit three stitches after completing each row of the chart pattern. WS rows are not charted and will be worked: K3, purl to last 3 sts, k3.

Work the chart until the body of the scarf is the length desired, ending on Row 32. Keep in mind that the decrease charts work to about 9" (23 cm) in length after blocking.

{ *note: The sample shown worked 9 chart repeats.*

Row 1: (RS) K20, (yo, k2tog) 15 times, k19.

Row 2 and all WS rows: K3, purl to last 3 sts, k3.

Row 3: K14, k3tog, (yo, k1) twice, (ssk, yo) 15 times, k1, (k1, yo) twice, sssk, k14.

Row 5: K12, k3tog, (k1, yo) twice, k3, (yo, k2tog) 15 times, k2, (yo, k1) twice, sssk, k12.

Row 7: K10, k3tog, k2, yo, k1, yo, k3, (ssk, yo) 15 times, k4, yo, k1, yo, k2, sssk, k10.

Row 9: K8, k3tog, k3, yo, k1, yo, k5, (yo, k2tog) 15 times, k4, yo, k1, yo, k3, sssk, k8.

Row 11: K6, k3tog, k4, yo, k1, yo, k5, (ssk, yo) 15 times, k6, yo, k1, yo, k4, sssk, k6.

Row 13: K20, (yo, k2tog) 15 times, k19.

Row 15: K19, (ssk, yo) 15 times, k20.

Row 17: K20, (yo, k2tog) 15 times, k19.

Row 19: K6, yo, k1, yo, sssk, k9, (ssk, yo) 15 times, k10, k3tog, yo, k1, yo, k6.

Row 21: K7, (yo, k1) twice, sssk, k8, (yo, k2tog) 15 times, k7, k3tog, (k1, yo) twice, k7.

Row 23: K8, yo, k1, yo, k2, sssk, k5, (ssk, yo) 15 times, k6, k3tog, k2, yo, k1, yo, k8.

Row 25: K9, yo, k1, yo, k3, sssk, k4, (yo, k2tog) 15 times, k3, k3tog, k3, yo, k1, yo, k9.

dappled leaves body chart

knit		yo		no stitch	
k2tog		k3tog		pattern repeat	
ssk		sssk			

Row 27: K10, yo, k1, yo, k4, sssk, k1, (ssk, yo) 15 times, k2, k3tog, k4, yo, k1, yo, k10.

Row 29: K20, (yo, k2tog) 15 times, k19.

Row 31: K19, (ssk, yo) times 15, k20.

Row 32: K3, purl to last 3 sts, k3.

Rep Rows 1–32 until the body of the scarf is the length desired, ending on Row 32.

BEGIN DAPPLED LEAVES DECREASE CHART A

Dappled Leaves Decrease chart A does not include the garter stitch border. Continue working the border as with the Body chart, knitting three stitches before the chart and three stitches after the chart.

WS rows are not charted and are worked: K3, purl to last 3 sts, k3.

Work chart A one time.

Row 1: (RS) K3, sssk, k14, (yo, k2tog) 3 times, k1, k3tog, yo, k1, yo, k2, (yo, cdd, yo), k2, yo, k1, yo, sssk, k2, (yo, k2tog) 3 times, k13, k3tog.

Even-numbered rows 2–12: K3, purl to last 3 sts, k3.

Row 3: K3, sssk, k11, (ssk, yo) twice, k2, k3tog, (k1, yo) twice, k3, (yo, cdd, yo), k3, (yo, k1) twice, sssk, k1, (ssk, yo) twice, k12, k3tog, k3.

Row 5: K3, sssk, k10, yo, k2tog, k1, k3tog, k2, yo, k1, yo, k4, (yo, cdd, yo), k4, yo, k1, yo, k2, sssk, k2, yo, k2tog, k9, k3tog, k3.

Row 7: K3, sssk, k9, k3tog, k3, yo, k1, yo, k5, (yo, cdd, yo), k5, yo, k1, yo, k3, sssk, k9, k3tog, k3.

Row 9: K3, sssk, k6, ssk, k9, k2tog, (yo, k1) 3 times, yo, ssk, k9, k2tog, k6, k3tog, k3.

Row 11: K3, sssk, k4, ssk, k7, k2tog, (k1, yo) 6 times, k1, ssk, k7, k2tog, k4, k3tog, k3.

BEGIN DAPPLED LEAVES DECREASE CHART B

Dappled Leaves Decrease chart B incorporates the garter stitch border. WS rows are charted.

Work chart B one time.

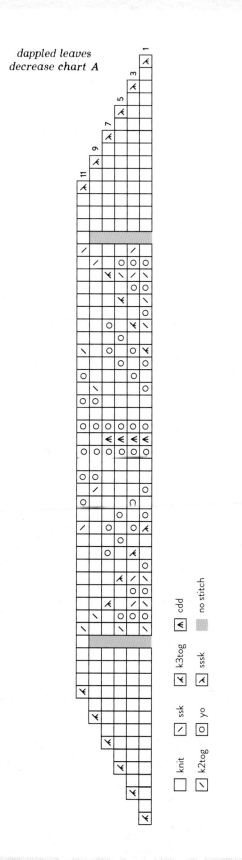

dappled leaves decrease chart A

The breezy center mesh panel creates a dappling effect that is set off perfectly by the alternating leaf edges and pointed ends.

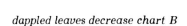

dappled leaves decrease chart B

	k on RS; p on WS		/	k2tog		O	yo		⼤	sssk
•	p on RW; k on WS		\	ssk		⼤	k3tog		⋏	cdd

Row 13: (RS) K2, sssk, k3, ssk, k5, k2tog, k2, yo, k1, yo, k2, (yo, cdd, yo), k2, yo, k1, yo, k2, ssk, k5, k2tog, k3, k3tog, k2.

Row 14: (WS) K2, purl to last 2 sts, k2.

Row 15: Sssk, k3, ssk, k3, k2tog, k3, yo, k1, yo, k3, yo, cdd, yo, k3, yo, k1, yo, k3, ssk, k3, k2tog, k3, k3tog.

Row 16: Purl across.

BEGIN DAPPLED LEAVES DECREASE CHART C

Dappled Leaves Decrease chart C does not include a garter stitch border (the border sts were decreased out in the prior chart).

WS rows are not charted. Purl across.

Work chart C one time.

Row 17: (RS) Sssk, k1, ssk, k1, k2tog, k4, yo, k1, yo, k4, yo, cdd, yo, k4, yo, k1, yo, k4, ssk, k1, k2tog, k1, k3tog.

Even-numbered rows 18–56: Purl across.

Row 19: Ssk, cdd, k9, k2tog, (yo, k1) 3 times, yo, ssk, k9, cdd, k2tog.

Row 21: K1, ssk, k7, k2tog, (k1, yo) 6 times, k1, ssk, k7, k2tog, k1.

Row 23: K1, ssk, k5, k2tog, k2, yo, k1, yo, k2, yo, cdd, yo, k2, yo, k1, yo, k2, ssk, k5, k2tog, k1.

Row 25: K1, ssk, k3, k2tog, k3, yo, k1, yo, k3, yo, cdd, yo, k3, yo, k1, yo, k3, ssk, k3, k2tog, k1.

Row 27: K1, ssk, k1, k2tog, k4, yo, k1, yo, k4, yo, cdd, yo, k4, yo, k1, yo, k4, ssk, k1, k2tog, k1.

Row 29: K1, cdd, k11, yo, cdd, yo, k11, cdd, k1.

Row 31: K1, ssk, k7, k2tog, k2, yo, k1, yo, k2, ssk, k7, k2tog, k1.

Row 33: K1, ssk, k5, k2tog, k3, yo, k1, yo, k3, ssk, k5, k2tog, k1.

Row 35: K1, ssk, k3, k2tog, k4, yo, k1, yo, k4, ssk, k3, k2tog, k1.

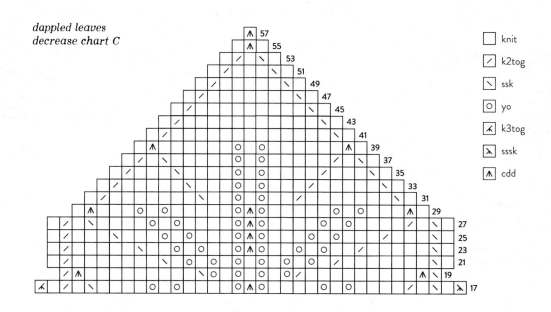

dappled leaves decrease chart C

□	knit
∕	k2tog
∖	ssk
○	yo
⋋	k3tog
⋌	sssk
⋀	cdd

Row 37: K1, ssk, k1, k2tog, k5, yo, k1, yo, k5, ssk, k1, k2tog, k1.

Row 39: K1, cdd, k6, yo, k1, yo, k6, cdd, k1.

Row 41: K1, ssk, k13, k2tog, k1.

Row 43: K1, ssk, k11, k2tog, k1.

Row 45: K1, ssk, k9, k2tog, k1.

Row 47: K1, ssk, k7, k2tog, k1.

Row 49: K1, ssk, k5, k2tog, k1.

Row 51: K1, ssk, k3, k2tog, k1.

Row 53: K1, ssk, k1, k2tog, k1.

Row 55: K1, cdd, k1.

Row 57: cdd.

Bind off.

Join yarn on WS at provisional cast-on.

Work the following WS row one time:
K3, purl to last 3 sts, k3.

Work as before, using the same number of Dappled Leaves Body repeats before beginning Dappled Leaves Decreases.

Finishing
BO all sts. Weave in ends and block.

PARTERRE WRAP

by amy gunderson

Parterre is a level space in a garden, occupied by flower beds; this wrap evokes their ornate beauty, in crisp linen held alongside a luxurious merino/silk blend. The first border of this rectangular stole is knit, followed by the shawl body; the shawl body stitches are then placed on a holder. The second border is knit and is then grafted to the shawl body stitches, giving a seamless and symmetric construction.

finished size
Width: 30¼" (77 cm); *Length:* 68" (172.5 cm)

yarn
Fingering weight (#1 super fine) (both yarns).

Shown here: Fibra Natura Whisper Lace
(70% superwash wool, 30% silk; 440 yd [402 m]/
1¾ oz [50 g]): 114 Lapis (A), 3 balls; Fibra
Natura Flax Lace (100% linen; 547 yd [500 m]/
3½ oz [100 g]): 107 Mineral (B), 2 hanks.

needles
Size U.S. 6 (4 mm): 32" (80 cm) circular (circ).

*Adjust needle size if necessary to
obtain the correct gauge.*

notions
Stitch markers; stitch holder; tapestry needle.

gauge
13 sts and 23 rows = 4" (10 cm) in Herringbone
Lace pattern with A and B held together.

17 sts and 23 rows = 4" (10 cm) in Scalloped
Edging with A and B held together.

{ *note: Listed gauge is after
aggressive blocking.*

notes
— It may be helpful to place stitch markers
between pattern repeats when working the
Scalloped Edging and Herringbone Lace
stitch patterns. Hold one strand of each
yarn together throughout this project.

Instructions

With one strand each of A and B held together, CO 129 sts.

Set-up row: (WS) K2, pm, p6, pm, purl to last 8 sts, pm, p6, pm, k2.

Beginning Border

*FIRST SCALLOPS SECTION

Row 1: (RS) K2, sl m, work Row 1 of Eyelet Columns chart to m, sl m, work Row 1 of Scalloped Edging chart to m (Scalloped Edging patt will be repeated 7 times across row), sl m, work Row 1 of Eyelet Columns chart to m, sl m, k2.

Row 2: (WS) K2, sl m, work Row 2 of Eyelet Columns chart to m, sl m, work Row 2 of Scalloped Edging chart to m, sl m, work Row 2 of Eyelet Columns chart to m, sl m, k2.

Cont as est'd through Row 8 of Scalloped Edging patt, then rep Rows 1–8 twice more.

FIRST GARTER RIDGE SECTION

Row 1: (RS) K2, sl m, work Row 1 of Eyelet Columns chart to m, sl m, work Row 1 of Garter Ridge chart to m, sl m, work Row 1 of Eyelet Columns chart to m, sl m, k2.

Row 2: (WS) K2, sl m, work Row 2 of Eyelet Columns chart to m, sl m, work Row 2 of Garter Ridge chart to m, sl m, work Row 2 of Eyelet Columns chart to m, sl m, k2.

Cont as est'd through Row 8 of Garter Ridge patt.

SECOND SCALLOPS SECTION

Row 1: (RS) K2, sl m, work Row 1 of Eyelet Columns chart to m, sl m, work Row 1 of Scalloped Edging chart to m, sl m, work Row 1 of Eyelet Columns chart to m, sl m, k2.

Row 2: (WS) K2, sl m, work Row 2 of Eyelet Columns chart to m, sl m, work Row 2 of Scalloped Edging chart to m, sl m, work Row 2 of Eyelet Columns chart to m, sl m, k2.

Cont as est'd through Row 8 of of Scalloped Edging patt, then rep Rows 1–8 once more.

scalloped edging chart

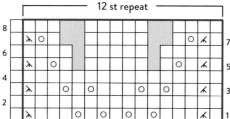

decrease scalloped edging chart

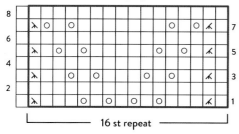

herringbone lace chart

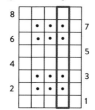

6 st repeat

garter ridge chart

eyelet columns chart

6 st panel

	k on RS; p on WS
•	p on RS; k on WS
/	k2tog
\	ssk
O	yo
⋏	k3tog
⋏	sssk
⋏	cdd: sl2, k1, p2sso
	no stitch
	pattern repeat

PECTINIDUS (*sea scallops*)

The scalloped borders are fun to knit and move the fabric in a dramatic direction. The herringbone lace in the body is easy to memorize & relaxing to knit.

DECREASE SECTION

Row 1: (RS) K2, sl m, work Row 1 of Eyelet Columns chart to m, sl m, work Row 1 of Decrease Scalloped Edging chart to m, sl m, work Row 1 of Eyelet Columns chart to m, sl m, k2.

Row 2: (WS) K2, sl m, work Row 2 of Eyelet Columns chart to m, sl m, work Row 2 of Decrease Scalloped Edging chart to m, sl m, work Row 2 of Eyelet Columns chart to m, sl m, k2.

Cont as est'd through Row 8 of of Decrease Scalloped Edging patt. 2 sts dec'd each rep—101 sts rem.

SECOND GARTER RIDGE SECTION

Work as for First Garter Ridge Section.**

Shawl Body

Row 1: (RS) K2, sl m, work Row 1 of Eyelet Columns chart to m, sl m, work Row 1 of Herringbone Lace chart to m (Herringbone Lace patt will be repeated 14 times across row), sl m, work Row 1 of Eyelet Columns chart to m, sl m, k2.

Row 2: (WS) K2, sl m, work Row 2 of Eyelet Columns chart to m, sl m, work Row 2 of Herringbone Lace chart to m, sl m, work Row 2 of Eyelet Columns chart to m, sl m, k2.

Cont as est'd, repeating Rows 1–4 of both patts until piece meas 68" (172.5 cm) from CO edge, ending with RS Row 3 of patts. Break yarn, place sts on spare needle.

Ending Border

Work as for Beginning Border from * to **.
Do not break yarn.

JOIN PIECES

Place final row of Ending Border against final row of Shawl Body. With RS facing, join the two sets of sts using Kitchener st, grafting the first and last 2 sts pwise, and rem sts kwise.

Finishing

Weave in ends. Run blocking wires along all sides of shawl. Pin to blocking board, stretching to open up lace. Wet or steam block.

puget tote

The Puget Tote is an all-season, multi-activity
carryall, perfect for the knitter who wants
to step out of their comfort zone for a bit of
a challenge. Great for day trips, this softly
structured, open-topped shoulder bag is knit
in moss stitch with a folded stockinette upper
edge. Instructions are also included for a simple
lining, making this bag both chic and practical.

BY ILLITILLI

finished size

10" (25.5 cm) wide, 4" (10 cm) deep, and 12" (30.5 cm) high, not including straps.

yarn

Sport weight (#2 fine).

Shown here: Appalachian Baby Design U.S. Organic Cotton Sport Weight (100% organic cotton; 194 yd [177 m]/3 oz [85 g]): undyed, 3 skeins.

needles

Size U.S. 2½ (3 mm): straight, 32" (80 cm) circular (cir), and set of double-pointed (dpn). Adjust needle size if necessary to obtain the correct gauge.

notions

Markers (m); stitch holders; tapestry needle; sewing needle and thread; sewing machine (optional); iron; lining fabric (see Notes): 1 piece 14½" (37 cm) × 30" (76 cm) for bag lining, 1 piece 8½" (21.5 cm) × 11¼" (28.5 cm) to cover base stiffener, 1 piece 6½" (16.5 cm) × 14" (35.5 cm) for interior pocket; heavyweight fusible facing (see Notes): 2 pieces 12" (30.5 cm) × 14" (35.5 cm), 2 pieces 4" (10 cm) × 10" (25.5 cm); plastic mesh stiffener (see Notes): 1 piece 4" (10 cm) × 10" (25.5 cm) ; ½" (1.3 cm) magnetic snap; unbleached cotton webbing strap, 2" (5 cm) wide × 3 yd (2.7 m) length (or desired length).

gauge

26 sts and 36 rows = 4" (10 cm) in St st.

notes

— The bottom of this bag is worked flat, starting with a provisional cast-on. Stitches are then picked up and the bag body is worked in the round. Each strap loop is backed with a short section of moss stitch worked flat from stitches held at the bottom of the loop and grafted to the bag body at the top of the loop. The faced lining includes a simple pocket and base stiffener.

— Lining fabric, facing, and base stiffener sizes are approximate; measure your blocked knitting to confirm required amounts.

— A sewing machine will be needed for finishing the bag lining.

stitch guide

MOSS STITCH (odd number of stitches)

Row 1: (WS) *K1, p1; rep from * to last st, k1.

Row 2: (RS) Rep Row 1.

Rows 3 and 4: *P1, k1; rep from * to last st, p1.

Rep Rows 1–4 for patt.

PURL CABLE CO

*Wyf, insert right needle from back to front between first 2 sts on left needle, wrap yarn as if to purl, draw yarn through to complete st and place new st kwise on left needle; rep from * for desired number of sts.

15-ST ONE-ROW BUTTONHOLE

Slip 1 pwise wyf, bring yarn to back. [Sl 1 pwise wyb, psso] 15 times. Place last st back on left needle, turn. Using the purl cable method (in this Stitch Guide), CO 16 sts onto left needle, turn. Bring yarn to back, transfer first st on left needle kwise to right needle and pass last CO st over it—buttonhole complete.

Bottom

With straight needles, and using a
provisional method, CO 28 sts.

Next row: (WS) Sl 1 pwise wyf, purl to end.

Next row: (RS) Sl 1 kwise wyb, knit to end.

Rep last 2 rows until piece measures 10"
(25.5 cm) from CO, ending with a WS row.

Sides

Next row: (RS) With dpn, sl 1 kwise wyb, k12, sl 2
pwise wyb, p1, place marker (pm), purl to end.

Turn work 90 degrees clockwise. With cir needle and
RS facing, pick up and knit 65 sts along side edge of
bag bottom, knitting into front leg of each slipped st,
and picking up additional sts as needed by knitting into
front and back legs of sts spaced evenly across length of
bag bottom, turn work 90 degrees clockwise—93 sts.

Remove waste yarn from provisional CO and
place 28 CO sts on dpn. With 2nd dpn, p12, pm,
p1, sl 2 pwise wyb, p1, pm, purl to end—121 sts.

Turn work 90 degrees clockwise. With working end of
cir needle, pick up and knit 65 sts along opposite side
edge of bag bottom, knitting into front leg of each
slipped st, and picking up additional sts as needed
by knitting into front and back legs of sts spaced
evenly across length of bag bottom—186 sts.

Turn work 90 degrees clockwise.
With dpn, p12. Pm for BOR.

{ ***note:*** *Work short sides from one dpn
onto another, and work long sides with cir
needle—needle cord will span across short
sides as you work.*

Body

Rnd 1: *P1, k2, p1, sl m, **k1, p1; rep from ** to 1 st before m, k1; rep from * to end.

Rnd 2: *P1, sl 2 pwise wyb, p1, sl m, **k1, p1; rep from ** to 1 st before m, k1; rep from * to end.

Rnd 3: *P1, k2, p1, sl m, **p1, k1; rep from ** to 1 st before m, p1; rep from * to end.

Rnd 4: *P1, sl 2 pwise wyb, p1, sl m, **p1, k1; rep from ** to 1 st before m, p1; rep from * to end.

Rnds 5–7: Rep Rnds 1–3.

Rnd 8: *P1, sl 2 pwise wyb, p1, sl m, [p1, k1] 8 times, sl 1 pwise wyf, bring yarn to back, return slipped st to left needle, place next 15 sts on holder, turn work.

Using the purl cable method (see Stitch Guide), CO 16 sts, turn work. Sl 1, pass last CO st over slipped st and return slipped st to left needle, [k1, p1] 13 times, k1, sl 1 pwise wyf, bring yarn to back, return slipped st to left needle, place next 15 sts on holder, turn work.

CO 16 sts, turn work.

Sl 1, pass last CO st over slipped st and return slipped st to left needle, [k1, p1] 8 times, sl m; rep from * to end.

Rnds 9–16: Rep Rnds 1–8.

Rnds 17 and 18: Rep Rnds 1 and 2.

Rnd 19: *P1, k2, p1, sl m, [p1, k1] 8 times, work 15-st one-row buttonhole (see Stitch Guide), return slipped st to left needle, [k1, p1] 13 times, k1, work buttonhole, return slipped st to left needle, [k1, p1] 8 times, sl m; rep from * to end.

Rnd 20: Rep Rnd 4.

Rep Rnds 1–4 until piece measures 8¾" (22 cm) from picked-up sts at bag bottom, ending with Rnd 3. Rep Rnds 8–19 once more.

Next rnd: *P1, sl 2 pwise wyb, p1, sl m, purl to m, sl m; rep from * to end.

Upper Edge

Rnd 1: P1, k3, sl m, knit to end.

Rnd 2: *K1, sl 2 pwise wyb, k1, sl m, knit to m, sl m; rep from * to end.

Rnd 3: Knit.

Rep Rnds 2 and 3 eight more times. Purl 1 rnd.

Inside Upper Edge

Rnd 1: Sl 1 pwise wyb, p2tog, k1, remove m, knit to next m, sl m, k1, p2tog, k1, remove m, knit to 1 st before m, sl 1 pwise wyb, remove m, return slipped st to left needle, ssk, pm—183 sts rem.

Rnd 2: P1, k2tog, knit to 1 st before m, sl 1 pwise wyb, remove m, return slipped st to left needle, ssk, pm, p1, k2tog, knit to end—180 sts rem.

Rnd 3: *P1, knit to m, sl m; rep from * to end.

Rep Rnd 3 until piece measures ⅞" (2 cm) from turning row.

BO all sts as foll:

*K2tog tbl, return st just worked to left needle; rep from * to last st, pick up front leg from first BO st and k2tog tbl, cut yarn and pull tail through rem st.

Strap Loop Backing

Place 15 held sts below strap loop on dpn. Working from inside of bag and with WS facing, join yarn and work 11 rows in Moss st (see Stitch Guide).

Rotate work 180 degrees, then using a spare dpn and cont with WS facing, join strap loop backing to bag as foll: Pick up and knit (using same yarn) 15 sts from CO row above strap loop. Rotate work 180 degrees again, break yarn, leaving a 12" (30.5 cm) tail, then graft live sts to picked-up sts using Kitchener st. Rep for each strap loop.

This tote is perfect takealong knitting for a ferry ride.

AEROPLANE VIEW OF THE PUGET SOUND AREA, WASHINGTON

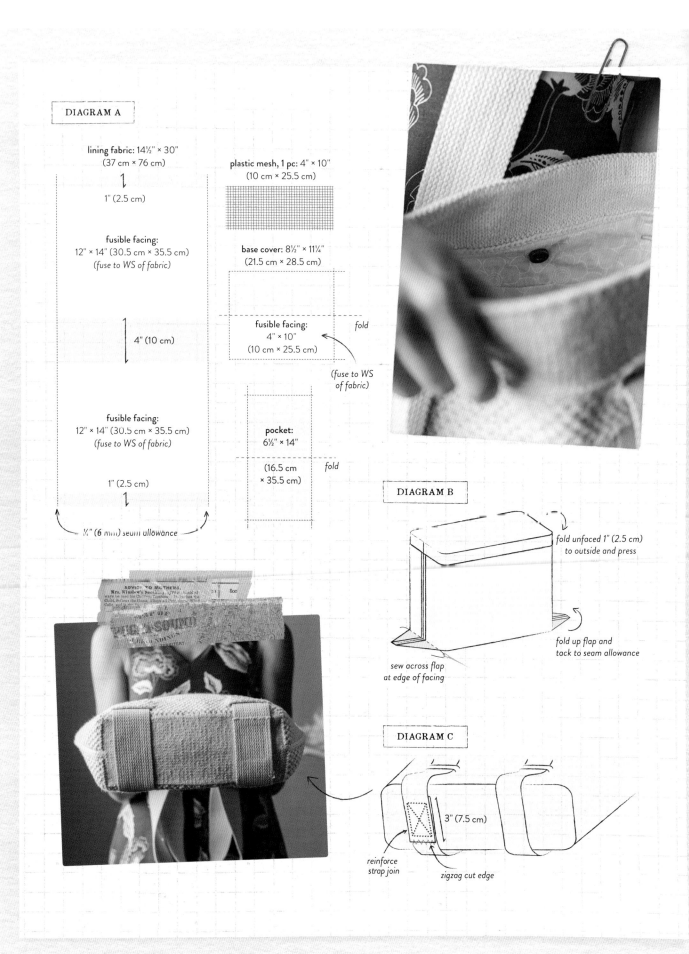

DIAGRAM A

lining fabric: 14½" × 30"
(37 cm × 76 cm)

1" (2.5 cm)

fusible facing:
12" × 14" (30.5 cm × 35.5 cm)
(fuse to WS of fabric)

4" (10 cm)

fusible facing:
12" × 14" (30.5 cm × 35.5 cm)
(fuse to WS of fabric)

1" (2.5 cm)

¼" (6 mm) seam allowance

plastic mesh, 1 pc: 4" × 10"
(10 cm × 25.5 cm)

base cover: 8½" × 11¼"
(21.5 cm × 28.5 cm)

fusible facing:
4" × 10"
(10 cm × 25.5 cm)
fold

(fuse to WS of fabric)

pocket:
6½" × 14"

(16.5 cm
× 35.5 cm)
fold

DIAGRAM B

fold unfaced 1" (2.5 cm)
to outside and press

fold up flap and
tack to seam allowance

sew across flap
at edge of facing

DIAGRAM C

3" (7.5 cm)

reinforce
strap join

zigzag cut edge

Finishing

Weave in ends. Wet block bag flat, folding upper edge to WS at turning rnd and inserting a 4" (10 cm) × 10" (25.5 cm) piece of corrugated cardboard, covered in plastic, into base for shaping.

CONSTRUCT LINING

Measure and cut lining fabric pieces, fusible facings, and plastic mesh, adjusting sizes as required to suit your blocked knitting (you may find it useful to construct a paper mockup to test for fit).

Using a hot, dry iron, fuse facings to WS of bag lining and base cover fabric as shown in Diagram A.

Fold pocket fabric in half with RS tog and sew side seams with a ¼" (6 mm) seam allowance. Turn RS out, fold 1" (2.5 cm) bottom seam allowance to inside, press and whipstitch closed.

Center pocket on one side of lining, about 4" (10 cm) down from top edge of facing on RS of lining, pin in place and topstitch side and bottom edges to attach to lining.

Center one half of magnetic snap on each side of RS of lining, about 3" (7.5 cm) down from top edge of facing, and install according to manufacturer's instructions.

Fold lining in half with RS tog, aligning snap closure, and sew side seams with a ¼" (6 mm) seam allowance.

Open lining and press corners flat, centering side seams on triangular point. Sew across these bottom points just to outside of facings, folding up resulting triangular flap and tacking it to side seams as shown in Diagram B—this forms squared ends of lining bottom.

Fold 1" (2.5 cm) of unfaced fabric at top of lining to outside (WS) and press. Fold fabric to cover base stiffener in half with RS tog and sew side and bottom seams with a ¼" (6 mm) seam allowance. Turn RS out, press, insert plastic mesh piece, fold 1" (2.5 cm) top seam allowance to inside and whipstitch closed.

Insert base stiffener, faced side up, into bottom of lining and pin in place. Tack each corner of base stiffener to corners of lining to secure it in place.

ATTACH LINING

Insert lining into knitted bag (WS of lining to WS of bag), aligning base stiffener with bag bottom and upper edge of lining with underside of turning row and pin in place. Check for alignment of bottom corners and side seams and whipstitch upper edge of lining to purl bumps just below turning row, making sure sewn sts are not visible from RS and do not distort knit fabric on outside of bag.

Fold upper edge of bag at turning rnd down over lining fabric and pin in place. Whipstitch BO edge of knit bag to lining.

ATTACH STRAP

Insert cotton webbing strap through strap loops as one continuous piece beginning at one side of bottom of bag, up through both strap loops on that side, leaving about 28" (71 cm) length for strap, down through opposite strap loops on same side, under bottom of bag, up through both strap loops on other side of bag, leaving about 28" (71 cm) length for strap, down through opposite strap loops on same side, then overlapping cut ends at bottom of bag by 3" (7.5 cm), making sure strap is not twisted.

Pin strap ends tog and sew using heavy thread, as shown in Diagram C. Use a sewing machine and zigzag stitch along cut edge of strap on each side of join to prevent fraying, or turn edge under and whipstitch folded edge by hand.

Pull strap back into place, making sure two straps are of equal length and join is located on bottom of bag, and pin in place. Using heavy thread, sew straps in place under each of top strap loops, working from inside of bag, catching lining, and making sure sewn sts do not catch outer knit strap loops.

SPRING SPROUT STOLE

Spring Sprout is a rectangular stole inspired by rows
of cultivated seedlings, worked from one short side to
the other. The garter stitch blocks seem to be tipped
at angles, but are simply worked in straight lines. The
simplicity of the stitch pattern makes the stole a perfect
project for relaxed knitting. The groups of increases and
decreases, which slant either to the left or right, pull the
garter squares one way or the other, creating a most
unusual pattern. The size of the stole can be altered
easily by working fewer or more repeats of the pattern.

by mone dräger

finished size
About 61" (155 cm) wide and 18½" (47 cm) long.

yarn
Fingering weight (#1 super fine).

Shown here: Purl Soho Field Linen (100% linen; 295 yd [270 m]/ 3½ oz [100 g]): #8520 Prairie Clover, 3 hanks.

needles
Size U.S. 2 (2.75 mm): 24" (60 cm) circular (cir) or straight needles.

Adjust needle size as necessary to obtain the correct gauge.

notions
Stitch markers (optional); tapestry needle.

gauge
19 sts and 27 rows = 4" (10 cm) in lace pattern, blocked.

notes
— Read all charts from bottom to top, odd-numbered RS rows from right to left, and even-numbered WS rows from left to right.

— To make it easier to keep track of the pattern, use stitch markers to mark each repeat.

— To alter the width of the stole, adjust the number of sts cast on by a multiple of 16 stitches. To alter the length of the stole, work fewer or more repeats of the 20-row lace pattern. For the best look, end with either Row 10 or Row 20.

The overall lace check pattern creates a fascinating appearance, yet it is easy to memorize and work.

Bottom Edging

Loosely CO 88 sts.

Knit 6 rows.

Body

Row 1: (RS) Working Row 1 of Spring Sprout chart, work first 12 sts at right edge of chart, rep next 16 sts 4 times, work rem 12 sts at left edge of chart.

Row 2: (WS) Working Row 2 of Spring Sprout chart, work first 12 sts at left edge of chart, rep next 16 sts 4 times, work rem 12 at right edge of chart.

Work Rows 3–20 of Spring Sprout chart as established, then rep Rows 1–20 nineteen more times.

Top Edging

Knit 6 rows.

Use the suspended bind-off method to BO all sts kwise.

Finishing

Weave in ends. Soak and block to measurements.

spring sprout chart

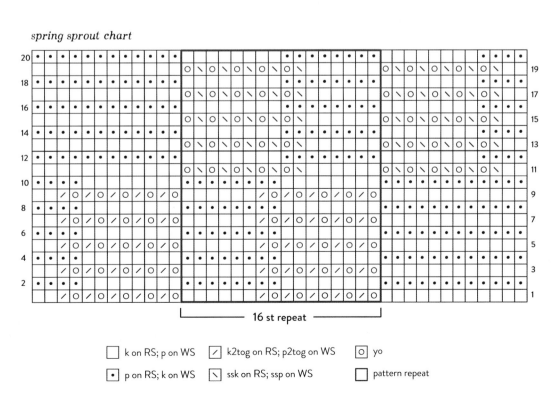

← 16 st repeat →

☐ k on RS; p on WS	✓ k2tog on RS; p2tog on WS	ⓞ yo
• p on RS; k on WS	◣ ssk on RS; ssp on WS	☐ pattern repeat

stonecrop
shawl

The delicate lace panel of this shawl was
inspired by the humble evergreen stonecrop
(sedum), an easy-to-grow group of succulent
plants that look great in any garden. Sedums
are vigorous and carefree, with a season of
interest lasting for more than half a year.
There's something simple and zen about the
appearance of succulents—from the sculpted
foliage to the deep green color of the leaves.

BY NINA TALBOT

finished size

About 54⅓" (138.5) wide and 70" (178 cm) long.

Hypotenuse: 89" (226 cm).

yarn

Light fingering weight (#1 super fine).

Shown here: YOTH Best Friend (75% cotton, 25% wool; 550 yd [502 m]/ 3½ oz [100 g]): #002 Olive, 2 skeins.

needles

Size U.S. 3 (3.25 mm): 32" (80 cm) circular (cir) to knit flat.

Adjust needle size as necessary to obtain the correct gauge.

notions

3 stitch markers (in different colors); tapestry needle.

gauge

21 sts and 28 rows = 4" (10 cm) in garter stitch.

21 sts and 22 rows = 4" (10 cm) in lace pattern.

notes

— This slightly elongated triangle shawl begins at the tip with 7 stitches. The lace panel grows out from the tip and continues on the right side up to the top edge. The main body and side borders are worked in garter stitch. The difference in gauge between lace and garter stitch makes this shawl slightly skewed inward. The increases occur only on the left side. At the top, the lace panel expands into a wide lace border. The piece is finished with a few rows of garter stitch.

— Lace charts A, B, and C: read charts from right to left on RS rows, and left to right on WS rows.

— Garter Edge Borders are not shown on the chart. All rows begin and end with k5 (edge stitches).

stitch guide

S1K2P

Slip 1 stitch from L to R needle as if to knit. K2tog from L needle. Pass the slipped stitch over the stitch you just worked—2 sts dec'd.

Instructions

CO 7 sts using the long-tail method
(see Techniques). Do not join.

Set-up row: (RS) K2, pm1, k5

Next row: (WS) Knit.

Shape Tip

Row 1: (RS) K1, k1f&b, sm1, knit to end—
1 st inc'd; 8 sts.

Row 2: (WS) Knit.

Row 3: Knit to 1 st before m1, k1f&b,
sm1, knit to end—1 st inc'd; 9 sts.

Row 4: Knit.

Rows 5–26: Rep Rows 3 and 4 eleven times—20 sts.

Begin Lace Chart A

note: This is where the lace chart begins.
The 5-stitch garter borders at the beginning and
end of each row are not shown on the chart.

Row 1: (RS) K5, pm2, k2, k2tog, k1,
yo, k4, k1f&b, sm1, k5—21 sts.

Rows 2–34 (all WS rows): K5, sm1,
purl across to m2, sm2, k5.

Row 3: K5, sm2, k1, k2tog, (k1, yo) twice,
k1, ssk, k2, k1f&b, sm1, k5—22 sts.

Row 5: K5, sm2, k2tog, k1, yo, k3, yo, k1,
ssk, k2, k1f&b, sm1, k5—23 sts.

Row 7: K5, sm2, yo, k1, ssk, k3, k2tog, k1,
yo, k3, k1f&b, sm1, k5—24 sts.

Row 9: K5, sm2, k1, yo, k1, ssk, k1, k2tog, (k1, yo)
twice, k1, ssk, k1, k1f&b, sm1, k5—25 sts.

Row 11: K5, sm2, k2, yo, k1, s1k2p, k1, yo, k3,
yo, k1, ssk, k1, k1f&b, sm1, k5—26 sts.

Row 13: K5, sm2, k2, k2tog, k1, yo, k5, k2tog,
k1, yo, k2, k1f&b, sm1, k5—27 sts.

Row 15: K5, sm2, [k1, k2tog, (k1, yo) twice,
k1, ssk] twice, k1f&b, sm1, k5—28 sts.

lace chart A

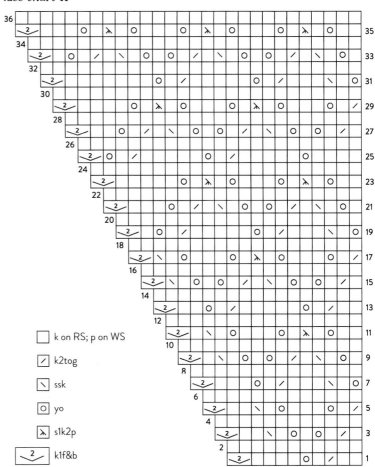

☐ k on RS; p on WS

☑ k2tog (/)

☑ ssk (\)

☑ yo (o)

☑ s1k2p (⅄)

☑ k1f&b (2)

Row 17: K5, sm2, k2tog, k1, yo, k3, yo, k1, s1k2p,
k1, yo, k3, yo, k1, ssk, k1f&b, sm1, k5—29 sts.

Row 19: K5, sm2, yo, k1, ssk, k3, k2tog, k1, yo,
k5, k2tog, k1, yo, k1, k1f&b, sm1, k5—30 sts.

Row 21: K5, sm2, (k1, yo, k1, ssk, k1, k2tog,
k1, yo) twice, k3, k1f&b, sm1, k5—31 sts.

Row 23: K5, sm2, k2, yo, k1, s1k2p, k1, yo, k3, yo,
k1, s1k2p, k1, yo, k5, k1f&b, sm1, k5—32 sts.

Row 25: K5, sm2, k4, (yo, k5, k2tog, k1) twice, yo, k1f&b, sm1, k5—33 sts.

Row 27: K5, sm2, [k1, k2tog, (k1, yo) twice, k1, ssk] twice, k1, k2tog, k1, yo, k2, k1f&b, sm1, k5—34 sts.

Row 29: K5, sm2, k2tog, (k1, yo, k3, yo, k1, s1k2p) twice, k1, yo, k4, k1f&b, sm1, k5—35 sts.

Row 31: K5, sm2, yo, k1, ssk, k3, k2tog, k1, yo, k5, k2tog, k1, yo, k7, k1f&b, sm1, k5—36 sts.

Row 33: K5, sm2, (k1, yo, k1, ssk, k1, k2tog, k1, yo) 3 times, k1, k1f&b, sm1, k5—37 sts.

Row 35: K5, sm2, k2, (yo, k1, s1k2p, k1, yo, k3) 3 times, k1f&b, sm1, k5—38 sts.

Row 36: K5, sm1, k3, pm3, purl across to m2, sm2, k5.

Begin Lace Chart B

note: Now there are three markers on the needles: m2 and m3 are used to define the lace panel and m1 to indicate where to k1f&b. Work the 5-stitch garter edge, then Lace chart B between m2 and m3, garter stitch between m3 and m1, make increase k1f&b before m1, finish with the 5-stitch garter border.

Row 1: (RS) K5, sm2, k2, (k2tog, k1, yo, k5) twice, k2tog, k1, yo, k4, sm3, work across to 1 st before m1, k1f&b, sm1, k5.

Row 2 and all WS rows: K5, sm1, knit to m3, sm3, purl across to m2, sm2, k5.

Row 3: K5, sm2, [k1, k2tog, (k1, yo) twice, k1, ssk] 3 times, k1, sm3, work across to 1 st before m1, k1f&b, sm1, k5.

Row 5: K5, sm2, k2tog, (k1, yo, k3, yo, k1, s1k2p) twice, k1, yo, k3, yo, k1, ssk, sm3, work across to 1 st before m1, k1f&b, sm1, k5.

Row 7: K5, sm2, yo, k1, ssk, k3, (k2tog, k1, yo, k5) twice, k2tog, k1, yo, sm3, work across to 1 st before m1, k1f&b, sm1, k5.

Row 9: K5, sm2, (k1, yo, k1, ssk, k1, k2tog, k1, yo) 3 times, k1, sm3, work across to 1 st before m1, k1f&b, sm1, k5.

Row 11: K5, sm2, k2, (yo, k1, s1k2p, k1, yo, k3) twice, yo, k1, s1k2p, k1, yo, k2, sm3, work across to 1 st before m1, k1f&b, sm1, k5.

Row 12: K5, sm1, knit to m3, sm3, purl across to m2, sm2, k5.

Rep Rows 1–12, 29 more times—218 sts.

Remove m3.

lace chart B

12																								
11		O	人	O			O	人	O			O	人	O	11
10																
9	O	╱		O	O	╱	╲	O	O	╱	╲	O	9
8												
7	O	╱		O	╱		O	╱	╲	O	╱	7
6												
5	╲	O		O	人	O		O	人	O		O	╱	5
4												
3	╲	O	O	╱	╲	O	O	╱	╲	O	O	╱	3
2												
1	O	╱		O	╱		O	╱	1

Legend:

□ k on RS; p on WS		○ yo	
╱ k2tog		人 s1k2p	
╲ ssk			

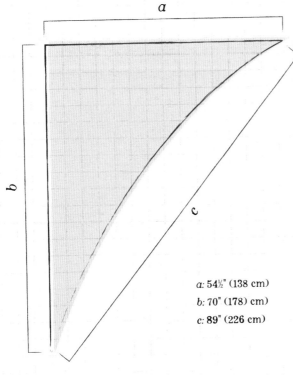

a: 54½" (138 cm)
b: 70" (178) cm)
c: 89" (226 cm)

Made in a lightweight fingering blend of cotton and wool, this triangle shawl becomes a great transitional piece throughout the seasons.

Begin Lace Chart C

note: The lace panel on the right expands into a lace border stretching all the way to the left edge. The 5-stitch garter borders at the beginning and end of each row are not shown on the chart.

Row 1: (RS) K5, sm2, work Lace chart C to rep line, work 8-st rep 24 times, work end of chart, sm1, k5.

Row 2 and all WS rows: K5, sm1, purl across to m2, k5.

Cont to work chart in this way through Row 36—236 sts.

Remove m2.

Row 37: (RS) Knit across to 1 st before m1, k1f&b, k5.

Row 38: (WS) K5, sm1, knit to end.

Rows 39—42: Rep Rows 37 and 38—239 sts.

Row 43: Loosely BO all sts using Stretchy Bind-off method.

Finishing

Weave in ends with tapestry needle.

Block and pin to measurements.

lace chart C

Chart legend:

- ☐ k on RS; p on WS
- ╱ k2tog
- ╲ ssk
- ⊙ yo
- ⋏ s1k2p
- ⌣2 k1f&b
- ☐ pattern repeat

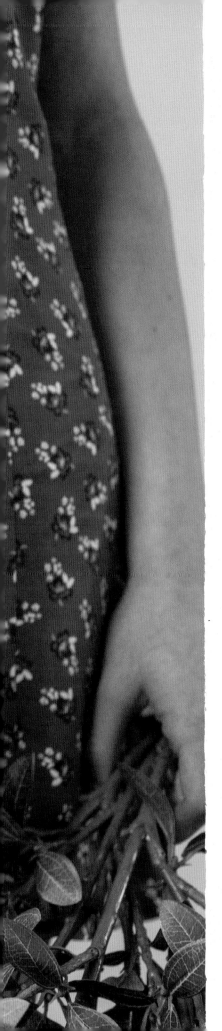

PINNATE TOTE

by illitilli

This casual linen tote features a graphic
slip-stitch chevron pattern inspired by pinnate
leaf forms, in which leaflets are arranged on
either side of a stem in pairs opposite each
other. The cool carryall is worked flat in pieces
and seamed. The strap is easy to make and
attach. It makes the perfect accessory for a
casual Saturday afternoon outing with friends.

finished size

About 12½" (31.5 cm) wide × 13½" (34.5 cm) high, with a 14" (35.5 cm) drop.

yarn

Aran weight (#4 medium).

Shown here: Quince and Co. Kestrel (100% organic linen; 76 yd [69 m]/1¾ oz [50g]): #512 Byzantium (A), 4 hanks; #500 Senza (B), 2 hanks.

needles

Size U.S. 4 (3.5 mm): pair of straight needles.

Size U.S. 7 (4.5 mm): pair of straight needles.

notions

Stitch marker; two 2" (5 cm) D-rings; tapestry needle; stitch holder or scrap yarn; cloth tape if desired.

gauge

22 sts and 31 rows = 4" (10 cm) in St st on size U.S. 4 (3.5 mm) needles.

23 sts and 39 rows = 4" (10 cm) in Slip Stitch Chevron pattern on size U.S. 7 (4.5 mm) needles.

notes

— This bag is worked flat in pieces and seamed. The side/bottom is worked in two pieces and grafted together. When using metal D-rings, you can reduce slippage by wrapping the straight portion of the ring with cloth tape, which will be hidden by the bag fabric.

stitch guide

SLIP STITCH CHEVRON

note: Slip all stitches purlwise with yarn in back on RS rows, and slip all stitches purlwise with yarn in front on WS rows.

Row 1: (RS) With B, k1, (sl 1, k2) to m, sm, sl 1, (k2, sl 1) to last st, k1.

Row 2: With B, k1, (sl 1, p2) to st before m, sl 1, sm, (p2, sl 1) to last st, k1.

Row 3: With A, k1, (k1, sl 1, k1) to m, sm, k1, (k1, sl 1, k1) to last st, k1.

Row 4: With A, k1, (p1, sl 1, p1) to st before m, p1, sm, (p1, sl 1, p1) to last st, k1.

Row 5: With B, k1, (k2, sl 1) to m, sm, k1, (sl 1, k2) to last st, k1.

Row 6: With B, k1, (p2, sl 1) to st before m, p1, sm, (sl 1, p2) to last st, k1.

Row 7: With A, rep Row 1.

Row 8: With A, rep Row 2.

Row 9: With B, rep Row 3.

Row 10: With B, rep Row 4.

Row 11: With A, rep Row 5.

Row 12: With A, rep Row 6.

Rep Rows 1–12 for pattern.

Front & Back Panels

With A and larger needles, CO 63 sts using the long-tail method.

Row 1: (WS) K1, p31, pm, purl to last st, k1.

Row 2: Begin Slip Stitch Chevron pattern starting with Row 1.

Work 9 complete repeats of Slip Stitch Chevron pattern.

Next row: (RS) With B, rep pattern Row 1.

Next row: (WS) With B, rep pattern Row 2.

GARTER EDGING

Row 1: (RS) Break B. Switch to smaller needles and using A, knit across all sts, removing the marker when you come to it.

Rows 2–4: Using A, knit.

Next row: Using A, loosely BO all sts using the knitted method.

Rep from CO to make a second panel.

Side/Bottom

With scrap yarn and smaller needle, provisionally CO 13 sts.

Row 1: (RS) With A, knit.

Row 2: (WS) Sl 1 pwise wyf, purl to end.

Row 3: Sl 1 kwise wyb, knit to end.

Rows 4–12: Rep Rows 2 and 3, ending after a WS row.

Next row: Thread CO edge through one D-ring, unravel provisional CO and place sts on spare needle. Fold strap over the D-ring with wrong sides together and the CO sts in back. *Insert right needle into first st on front needle and first st on back needle, k2tog; rep from * to end to create a folded hem around the D-ring.

Next row: (WS) Sl 1 pwise wyf, purl to end.

Next row: (RS) Sl 1 kwise wyb, knit to end.

Rep these two rows until work measures 18¼" (46.5 cm) from the folded top edge, ending after a WS row. Cut yarn and place live sts on scrap yarn or spare needle to hold. Repeat from provisional CO for the second half of the side/bottom panel, ending after a RS row. Cut yarn to leave a 12" (30.5 cm) tail—use this tail to graft the two halves together using Kitchener stitch.

Strap

With A and smaller needle, CO 9 sts, leaving a 12" (30.5 cm) tail of working yarn at beginning of your CO.

Row 1: (RS) K1, sl 1 pwise wyf, k5, sl 1 pwise wyf, k1.

Row 2: (WS) Sl 1 pwise wyf, k1, sl 1 pwise wyf, k3, sl 1 pwise wyf, k1, sl 1 pwise wyf.

Rep these 2 rows until the strap measures 28" (71 cm) when vigorously stretched. Bind off all sts and cut working yarn, leaving a 12" (30.5 cm) tail.

Finishing

Attach the strap by threading one end through each D-ring, making sure not to twist, and folding the edge over the D-ring to make a ½" (1.3 cm) folded hem. Use the 12" (30.5 cm) yarn tail to sew the hem to the WS of the strap using a whipstitch. Weave in ends.

Choose an accent color for all your favorite florals, and make a veritable bouquet of bags!

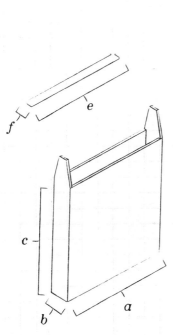

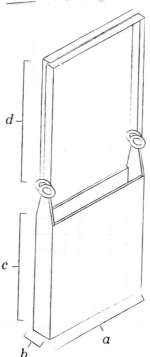

a: 12½" (32 cm)

b: 2¼" (5.5 cm)

c: 13½" (34.5 cm)

d: 14" (35.5 cm)

e: 28" (71 cm)

f: 1½" (3.8 cm)

GARMENTS

tees : tunics : tank : vest : tops

driftwood

lace leaf

TAOS

villandry

icicle drop

trellis

yellow ivy

arizona

puck's

seabrook

kenno

trellis tank

The Trellis Tank uses line and texture to convey the impression of length, with a promise of texture at the top. It has a unique neckline with crochet lacing and a zigzag edge. Stockinette stitch, reverse stockinette, and twisted knit ribbing on the yoke frame the zigzag neckline. Six body sections outlined by faux seams give the body structure, and the slight A-line shape follows body contours. The yarn contains two natural fibers: cotton and hemp, combined with modal. The hemp will become softer with each washing, while the modal imparts a great drape.

BY MARGARET HOLZMANN

finished size
Bust circumference: about 32 (36, 40, 44, 48)"
(81.5 [91.5, 101.5, 112, 122] cm).

yarn
DK weight (#3 light).

Shown here: Elsebeth Lavold Hempathy (41%
cotton, 34% hemp, 25% modal; 153 yd [140 m]/
3½ oz [100 g]): #51 charcoal, 5 (6, 6, 7, 8) skeins.

needles
Size U.S. 5 (3.75 mm): 24" (60 cm) circular (cir).

*Adjust needle size if necessary to
obtain the correct gauge.*

notions
Markers (m); stitch holders; tapestry
needle; size U.S. D/3 (3.25 mm) and
size U.S. 7 (4.5 mm) crochet hooks.

gauge
20 sts and 29 rows = 4" (10 cm) in St st on
size U.S. 5 needles or size to obtain gauge.

23 sts and 32 rows = 4" (10 cm) in Twisted
Knit Ribbing on size U.S. 5 needles.

notes
— The tank is worked from bottom to underarms
in the round and then separated for Front and
Back and worked back and forth. Six faux seams
are established on the first row. Each is worked
as 3 purl sts and appears as a reverse stockinette
st column on the RS of the garment. These are
referred to as "faux seams" in the instructions.
When the garment is complete, the centerline of
the faux seams is added with a crochet slip stitch,
and the diagonal lines at the neck are created with
crochet chain reinforced with single crochet.

stitch guide

**TWISTED KNIT RIBBING WORKED
BACK AND FORTH (odd number of sts)**
Row 1: (RS) *K1 tbl, p1; rep from * to last st, k1 tbl.

Row 2: (WS) P1 tbl, *k1, p1 tbl; rep from * across.

Rep Rows 1 and 2 for patt.

Body

CO 184 (204, 224, 244, 264) sts.

*P3, k25 (30, 35, 40, 45), p3, k33, p3, k25 (30, 35, 40, 45); rep from * once. Join in a circle, untwisting sts.

Work 23 (24, 24, 24, 25) rnds even.

Right-leaning dec rnd: *P3, k2tog, knit to next faux seam; rep from * to end of rnd—6 sts dec'd—178 (198, 218, 238, 258) sts.

Work 23 (24, 24, 24, 25) rnds even.

Left-leaning dec rnd: *P3, knit to 2 sts before next faux seam, ssk; rep from * to end of rnd—6 sts dec'd—172 (192, 212, 232, 252) sts.

Rep last 48 (50, 50, 50, 52) rnds once—12 sts dec'd—160 (180, 200, 220, 240) sts.

Work even until piece measures 17 (17¼, 17½, 17¾, 18). (43 [44, 44.5, 45, 45.5] cm) from CO, ending 1 (3, 3, 5, 6) sts before end of rnd.

BO next 5 (9, 9, 13, 15) sts for Left Armhole, work to 1 (3, 3, 5, 6) st(s) before 4th faux seam while maintaining established patterns, BO next 5 (9, 9, 13, 15) sts for Right Armhole, placing 75 (81, 91, 97, 105) worked sts on holder for Front.

Back

🍃 *note: Worked back and forth.*

Place m on either side of center 43 sts.

WS rows: Purl to first m, sm, knit to 2nd m, sm, purl to end.

RS rows: Knit to first m, sm, purl to 2nd m, sm, knit to end.

Rows 1–8: Rep WS and RS rows 4 times while dec 1 st each armhole edge every RS row 1 (1, 2, 2, 5) time(s)—73 (79, 87, 93, 95) sts rem.

Row 9: (WS) Purl to first m, sm, k6, [ptbl, k1] 15 times, ptbl, k6, sm, purl to end.

Move first m back 8 sts. Move 2nd m forward 8 sts so that the center 59 sts are between m's.

Row 10: (RS) Knit to 1st m, sm, p14, [ktbl, p1] 15 times, ktbl, p14, sm, knit to end.

Row 11: Purl to first m, sm, k14, [ptbl, k1] 15 times, ptbl, k14, sm, purl to end.

Rows 12–17: Rep Rows 10 and 11.

Row 18: Knit to first m, sm, p6, [ktbl, p1] 23 times, ktbl, p6, sm, knit to end. Remove m.

Row 19: P0 (2, 6, 9, 10), k13 (14, 14, 14, 14), [ptbl, k1] 23 times, ptbl, k13 (14, 14, 14, 14), p0 (2, 6, 9, 10).

Row 20: K0 (2, 6, 9, 10), p13 (14, 14, 14, 14), [ktbl, p1] 23 times, ktbl, p13 (14, 14, 14, 14), k0 (2, 6, 9, 10).

Rows 21–25: Rep Rows 19 and 20.

Row 26: K0 (2, 6, 9, 10), p13 (14, 14, 14, 14), [ktbl, p1] 9 times, ktbl, BO 9, placing 32 (35, 39, 42, 43) sts worked on holder for Right Shoulder, [ktbl, p1] 9 times, ktbl, p13 (14, 14, 14, 14), k0 (2, 6, 9, 10)—32 (35, 39, 42, 43) sts for Left Shoulder.

LEFT SHOULDER

Row 27: (WS) P0 (2, 6, 9, 10), k5 (6, 6, 6, 6), [ptbl, k1] 13 times, ptbl.

Row 28: (RS) [Ktbl, p1] 13 times, ktbl, purl to end.

Row 29: K5 (8, 12, 15, 16), [ptbl, k1] 13 times, ptbl.

Rows 30–33: Rep Rows 28 and 29.

Row 34: Rep Row 28.

Row 35: K5 (8, 12, 15, 16), [ptbl, k1] 9 times, ptbl, BO 8—24 (27, 31, 34, 35) sts. Tie off and cut yarn. Turn and reattach yarn.

Row 36: [Ktbl, p1] 11 (13, 13, 13, 13) times, ktbl, p1 (0, 4, 7, 8).

Row 37: K1 (0, 4, 7, 8), *ptbl, k1; rep from * to last st, ptbl.

Rows 38–43: Rep Rows 36 and 37.

Row 44: BO 8, [ktbl, p1] 7 (9, 9, 9, 9) times, ktbl, p1 (0, 4, 7, 8)—16 (19, 23, 26, 27) sts.

Rows 45–52: Cont working established Twisted Knit Ribbing.

Row 53: Work Twisted Knit Ribbing to last 8 sts, BO 8—8 (11, 15, 18, 19) sts.

Tie off and cut yarn. Turn and reattach yarn.

Rows 54–61: Cont working established Twisted Knit Ribbing.

Sizes XS, S, M
Place rem 8 (11, 15, -, -) sts on holder.

Sizes L, 1X only

Row 62: BO 8, work Twisted Knit Ribbing to end— - (-, -, 10, 11) sts.

Work 8 rows in established Twisted Knit Ribbing.

Place rem — - (-, -, 10, 11) sts on holder.

RIGHT SHOULDER

Transfer sts for Right Shoulder to needle. Attach yarn and start on WS—32 (35, 39, 42, 43) sts.

Row 27: (WS) [Ptbl, k1] 13 times, ptbl, k5 (6, 6, 6, 6), purl to end.

Row 28: (RS) P5 (8, 12, 15,16), [ktbl, p1] 13 times, ktbl.

Row 29: [Ptbl, k1] 13 times, ptbl, knit to end.

Rows 30–33: Rep Rows 28 and 29.

Row 34: Rep Row 28.

Row 35: BO 8, [ptbl, k1] 9 times, ptbl, knit to end—24 (27, 31, 34, 35) sts.

Row 36: P1 (0, 4, 7, 8), *ktbl, p1; rep from * to last st, ktbl.

Row 37: [Ptbl, k1] 11 (13, 13, 13, 13) times, ptbl, k1 (0, 4, 7, 8).

Rows 38–43: Rep Rows 36 and 37.

Row 44: P1 (0, 4, 7, 8), *ktbl, p1; rep from * to last 8 sts, BO 8—16 (19, 23, 26, 27) sts. Tie off and cut yarn. Turn and reattach yarn.

Rows 45–52: Cont working established Twisted Knit Ribbing.

Row 53: BO 8, *ptbl, k; rep from * to last st, ptbl—8 (11, 15, 18, 19) sts.

Rows 54–61: Cont working established Twisted Knit Ribbing.

Sizes XS, S, M only

Place rem 8 (11, 15, -, -) sts on holder.

Sizes L, 1X only

Row 62: Work Twisted Knit Ribbing to last 8 sts, BO 8—10 (11) sts. Tie off and cut yarn. Turn and reattach yarn.

Work 8 rows in established Twisted Knit Ribbing.

Place rem 10 (11) sts on holder.

Front

Transfer sts for Front from holder to needle—75 (81, 91, 97, 105) sts.

Attach yarn at right underarm and start work on WS. Rep as for Back, leaving sts on needle when complete.

Finishing

Match Right Front and Right Back Shoulder seams and graft tog using Kitchener stitch. Rep for Left Front and Left Back Shoulder seams.

NECKLINE EDGING

Using size D/3 (3.25 mm) crochet hook and starting at the left corner of the back neck, make 6 sc in each vertical edge, 2 sc in the corner, and 6 sc in each horizontal edge. Cont for the Left Front neckline as shown in Diagram A, creating a longer vertical edge of 12 sc on each side, until the center 9 sts of the Front. Make 8 sc across the center front, then continue around to the center back, making 8 sc in the center back. See Diagram A for clarification.

NECKLINE STRAPS
Right Strap

Attach yarn to the left bottom corner of the center front square opening. With smaller crochet hook, *ch 9, sl st in the crochet point of the next corner of the Right Front neckline; rep from * 2 (2, 2, 3, 3) times, ch 9, sl st in Right Shoulder seam at edge, **ch 9, sl st in next back, right neck neckline corner; rep from ** 2 (2, 2, 3, 3) times, ch 9, sl st in left bottom corner of center back square opening, sc 1 in next st, ch 1, turn, and sc in each ch back to shoulder, skip 1 chain to turn corner, then sc in each ch back to start. See diagram B for clarification.

Left Strap

Attach yarn to the right bottom corner of the center back square opening. With smaller crochet hook, *ch 9, sl st in the crochet point of the next corner of the Left Back neckline; rep from * 2 (2, 2, 3, 3) times, ch 9, sl st in Left Shoulder seam at edge, *ch 9, sl st in next front, left neck neckline corner; rep from * 2 (2, 2, 3, 3) times, ch 9, sl st in right bottom corner of center front square opening, sc 1 in next st, ch 1, turn, and sc in each ch back to shoulder, skip 1 chain to turn corner, then sc in each chain back to start. See diagram C for clarification.

DIAGRAM A

back

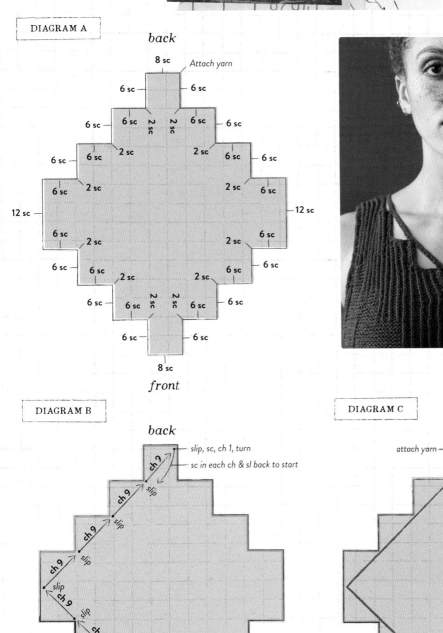

Attach yarn

8 sc

6 sc — — 6 sc

6 sc — 6 sc — 2 sc — 2 sc — 6 sc — 6 sc

6 sc — 6 sc — 2 sc — — 2 sc — 6 sc — 6 sc

6 sc — 2 sc — — 2 sc — 6 sc

12 sc — — 12 sc

6 sc — 2 sc — — 2 sc — 6 sc

6 sc — 6 sc — 2 sc — — 2 sc — 6 sc — 6 sc

6 sc — 6 sc — 2 sc — 2 sc — 6 sc — 6 sc

6 sc — — 6 sc

8 sc

front

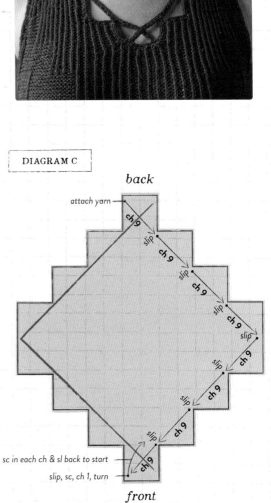

DIAGRAM B

back

slip, sc, ch 1, turn

ch 2

sc in each ch & sl back to start

ch 9 — slip

ch 9 — slip

ch 9 — slip

ch 9 — slip

slip

ch 9

slip

ch 9

slip

ch 9

slip

ch 9

attach yarn

front

DIAGRAM C

back

attach yarn

ch 9

slip

ch 9

slip

ch 9

slip

ch 9

slip

slip

ch 9

slip

ch 9

slip

ch 9

sc in each ch & sl back to start

ch 9

slip, sc, ch 1, turn

front

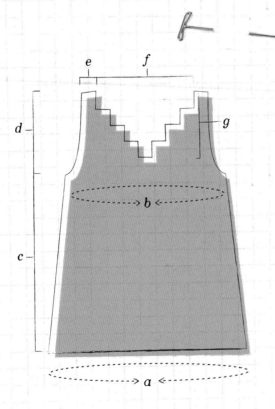

a: 36¾ (40¾, 44¾, 48¾, 52¾)"
(93.5 [103.5, 113.5, 124, 134] cm)

b: 32 (36, 40, 44, 48)"
(81.5 [91.5, 101.5, 112, 122] cm)

c: 17(17¼, 17½, 17¾, 18)"
(43 [44, 44.5, 45, 45.5] cm)

d: 7¾ (7¾, 7¾, 8¾, 8¾)"
(19.5 [19.5, 19.5, 22, 22] cm)

e: 1½ (2, 2½, 1¾, 2)"
(3.8 [5, 6.5, 5, 4.5, 5] cm)

f: 10 (10, 10, 12¾, 12¾)"
(25.5 [25.5, 25.5, 32.5, 32.5] cm)

g: 3½ (3½, 3½, 4½, 4½)"
(9 [9, 9, 11.5, 11.5] cm)

A LITTLE trellis stood
beside my head,
And all the tiny
fruitage of its vine
Fashioned a shadowy
cover to my bed,
And I was madly drunk
on shadow wine !

– from Djuna Barnes, "Shadows"

ARMHOLE EDGING

Left Armhole

Attach yarn to Left Armhole at the back where the Rev St st pattern starts. Sc in selvedge sts of armhole at rate of 4 sc to every 5 selvedge sts. Crochet a complete rnd, then continue sc at the same rate until the start of the stockinette area of the Front is reached, sl st in the next selvedge st, then tie off.

Right Armhole

Rep as for Left Armhole, attaching yarn at bottom of Rev St st area on Front, completing full rnd, and ending at bottom of Rev St st area on Back.

FAUX SEAMS FINISHING

Using the larger crochet hook and with RS facing, draw a double strand of yarn through the edge of the hem at the left side at the center of the 3 Rev St sts. Tie the yarn to the edge, draw up a loop in the middle Rev St st at the hem, *insert the hook front to back through the next center purl st and loop the yarns over the hook and draw yarns to front, through the existing loop on the hook, adjust tension. Skip 2 purl sts and insert the hook front to back through the 2nd purl st and loop the yarns over the hook and draw yarns to front, through the existing loop on the hook, adjust tension; rep from * until the top of the Rev St st column is reached. Cut yarn and pull through last loop. Pull yarn end through to back of work.

Rep faux finishing for the other 5 faux seams.

HEM EDGING

Using smaller crochet hook and with RS facing, attach yarn to left side seam hem. Sc in each hem st. To complete rnd, sl st in first st, tie off, and cut yarn.

Block to measurements and weave in ends.

ICICLE DROP TEE

With a gentle nod to the icicles that
hang from branches in winter, this tee
is a perfect layering piece, with simple
shape and a subtle shine. Endlessly
versatile, it's the perfect top for a day at
the beach or a night on the town. The
inset shoulder adds interest and texture.

by adrienne larsen

finished size

Bust circumference: About 34 (38¼, 41¾, 46¼, 50)" (86.5 [97, 106, 117.5, 127] cm)

yarn

Sport weight (#2 fine).

Shown here: Shibui Knits Twig (46% linen/42% recycled silk /12% wool; 190 yd [174 m]/1¾ oz [50 g]): Ash, 7 (9, 9, 10, 11) skeins.

needles

Size U.S. 3 (3.25 mm): 16" (40 cm) and 24" (60 cm) circular (cir) needles.

Adjust needle size as necessary to obtain the correct gauge.

notions

Markers (m); stitch holder; size U.S. C/2 (2.75 mm) crochet hook.

gauge

23 sts and 38 rows = 4" (10 cm) in St st.

notes

Tee is picked up from shoulder inset and knitted top down in the round.

stitch guide

LEFT LIFTED INCREASE (LLI)

Insert your left needle from front to back through the stitch two stitches below the last stitch on the right needle. Knit.

RIGHT LIFTED INCREASE (RLI)

Insert your right needle from back to front through the stitch below the next stitch on the left needle, slip stitch purlwise to left needle. Knit.

Shoulder Inset

With shorter needle, CO 24 (26, 28, 30, 32) sts.

Row 1: (WS) K1, purl to last st, k1.

Row 2: P1, knit to last st, p1.

Work even for 3 (3¼, 3½, 3¼, 3)" (7.5 [8.5, 9, 8.5, 7.5] cm), ending with a WS row.

Next row: P1, k10 (11, 12, 13, 14), p1, turn.

Place remaining 12 (13, 14, 15, 16) sts on holder. Continue in pattern for 8 (9½, 10½, 11¼, 11½)" (20.5 [24, 26.5, 28.5, 29] cm), ending with a RS row. Break yarn and place sts on holder.

Attach yarn to unworked second half of sts.

Next row: P1, k10 (11, 12, 13, 14), p1, turn.

Continue in pattern for 8 (9½, 10½, 11¼, 11½)" (20.5 [24, 26.5, 28.5, 29] cm), ending with WS row.

Next row: (RS) P1, knit to end of row, place sts from holder on needles and knit to last st, p1—24 (26, 28, 30, 32) sts.

Row 1: (WS) K1, purl to last st, k1.

Row 2: P1, knit to last st, p1.

Repeat last 2 rows for 3 (3¼, 3½, 3¼, 3)" (7.5 [8.5, 9, 8.5, 7.5] cm). BO.

Front

With longer needles and RS facing, pick up and knit 81 (91, 101, 101, 101) sts along long edge of shoulder inset.

Row 1 and all WS rows: K1, purl to last st, k1.

Row 2: P1, k4, *yo, k2tog, k3; rep from * to last 7 sts, yo, k2tog, k4, p1.

Row 4: P1, *k3, ssk, yo; rep from * to last 5 sts, k4, p1.

Rows 6 and 8: Rep Rows 2 and 4.

Row 10: Rep Row 2.

Row 12: P1, k3, *ssk, yo, k8; rep from * to last 8 sts, k1, ssk, yo, k4, p1.

Row 14: P1, k4, *yo, k2tog, k8; rep from * to last 6 sts, yo, k2tog, k3, p1.

Rows 16 and 18: Rep Rows 12 and 14.

Row 20: Rep Row 12.

Row 22: P1, knit to last st, p1.

Rep Rows 21 and 22 until piece measures 4¾ (5¼, 5½, 5¾, 6¼)" (12 [13.5, 14, 14. 5, 16] cm) from picked-up edge, ending with a WS row. Put sts on holder.

Back

Work as for Front. Do not place sts on holder.

Body

Rnd 1: Knit across 81 (91, 101, 101, 101) Back sts, CO 8 (9, 9, 16, 21) sts, pm, CO 9 (10, 10, 16, 22) sts, knit across 81 (91, 101, 101, 101) Front sts, CO 8 (9, 9, 16, 21) sts, pm for beg of rnd, CO 9 (10, 10, 16, 22) sts—196 (220, 240, 266, 288) sts.

Rnd 2: Knit to end of rnd. Cont in St st for 7 (6, 7, 7, 8) rows.

Dec rnd: *K2tog, knit to 2 sts before marker, ssk: rep from * around—4 sts dec'd.

Continue in St st, while working Dec rnd every 8 (7, 8, 8, 9) rows 5 (1, 2, 4, 1) more time(s), then every 0 (6, 7, 7, 8) rows 0 (6, 4, 2, 5) times—172 (188, 212, 238, 260) sts.

Work even for 2" (5 cm).

Inc rnd: *RLI, knit to marker, LLI; rep from * around—4 sts increased.

Cont in St st while working Inc rnd every 9 (8, 10, 9, 6) rows 4 (5, 6, 6, 6) times, then every 10 (9, 0, 10, 8) rows 2 (2, 0, 1, 3) time(s)—200 (220, 240, 270, 300) sts.

Rnd 1: *K6, yo, k2tog, k2; rep from * around.

Rnd 2 and all even-numbered rows: Knit.

Rnd 3: *K5, ssk, yo, k3; rep from * around

Rnds 5 and 7: Rep Rnds 1 and 3.

Rnd 9: Rep Rnd 1.

Rnd 11: *Ssk, yo, k3; rep from * around.

Rnd 13: *K1, yo, k2tog, k2; rep from * around.

Rnds 15 and 17: Rep Rnds 11 and 13.

Rnd 19: Rep Rnd 11.

Rnd 20: Knit.

Rnd 21: Purl.

Rnd 22: Knit.

BO all sts purlwise.

Sleeve Edging

With shorter needles and RS facing, pick up and knit 17 (19, 19, 32, 43) sts along underarm, 27 (30, 33, 35, 36) sts to shoulder inset, 22 (24, 26, 28, 30) sts along shoulder inset, 27 (30, 33, 35, 36) sts to underarm, pm for beg of rnd—93 (103, 111, 130, 145) sts.

Rnd 1: Knit.

Cont knitting even for 1" (2.5 cm).

Next rnd: Purl.

Knit even for 1" (2.5 cm).

BO all sts. Fold in half and stitch down as hem.

Finishing

Work single crochet edging around neck. Block to schematic measurements and weave in ends.

why are some icicles long some short?

— Ueshima Onitsura (1660–1738), tr. R. H. Blyth

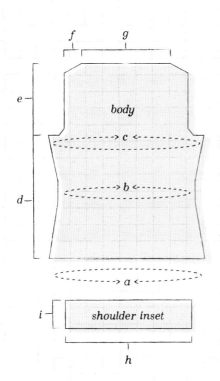

a: 36 (40, 44, 48, 52)"
(91.5 [101.5, 112, 122, 132] cm)

b: 30 (32¾, 36¾, 41½, 45¼)"
(76 [83, 93.5, 105.5, 115] cm)

c: 34 (38¼, 41¾, 46¼, 50)"
(86.5 [97, 106, 117.5, 127] cm)

d: 15 (15½, 16, 16½, 17)"
(38 [39.5, 40.5, 42, 43] cm)

e: 4¾ (5¼, 5¾, 6, 6¼)"
(12 [13.5, 14.5, 15, 16] cm)

f: 3 (3¼, 3½, 3¼, 3)"
(7.5 [8.5, 9, 8.5, 7.5] cm)

g: 8 (9½, 10½, 11¼, 11½)"
(20.5 [24, 26.5, 28.5, 29] cm)

h: 14 (15¾, 17½, 17½, 17½)"
(35.5 [40, 44.5, 44.5, 44.5] cm)

i: 4¼ (4½, 4¾, 5¼, 5½)"
(11 [11.5, 12, 13.5, 14] cm)

yellow ivy
halter top

Knit in an irresistible silver/goldenrod color
combination, Yellow Ivy comes to glorious
life—a lightweight and lovely seamless
halter-neck top with A-line shaping, a lacy
yoke in a contrasting color, and garter stitch
shoulder straps. Worked in a combination
of cotton and linen, it is the perfect
warm-weather item to knit and wear.

BY PETRA MACHOVÁ KOUŘILOVÁ

finished size

Bust circumference: about 28 (32, 36, 40, 44)" (71 [81.5, 91.5, 101.5, 112] cm.

yarn

DK weight (#3 light).

Shown here: BC Garn Allino (50% cotton, 50% linen; 137 yd [125 m]/ 1¾ oz [50 g]): 06 Silver (MC), 3 (4, 4, 5, 5) balls; 21 Copper (CC), 2 (2, 2, 3, 3) balls.

needles

Size U.S. 4 (3.5 mm).

Size U.S. 2½ (3 mm).

Adjust needle sizes as necessary to obtain the correct gauge.

notions

Stitch holder or scrap yarn; 5 stitch markers (4 for A-line increases + 1 in different style for BOR); tapestry needle.

gauge

22 sts and 29 rows = 4" (10 cm) in St st on size U.S. 4 (3.5 mm) needles.

22 sts and 36 rows = 4" (10 cm) in lace pattern on size U.S. 2½ (3 mm) needles

notes

The top is intended to be close fitting in the bust and loose fitting in the waist-and-hips area. Choose a size with about 0–3" [0–7.5 cm] of negative ease at full bust.

stitch guide

STOCKINETTE STITCH in the round:
Knit every round.

GARTER STITCH in the round:
Knit 1 round, purl 1 round.

CENTERED DOUBLE DECREASE (CDD)
Slip 2 stitches together knitwise, knit 1, pass 2 slipped stitches over—2 sts dec'd.

MAKE 1 LEFT (M1L)
Using left-hand needle, lift the bar between the stitch just worked and the next stitch from the front, knit this stitch through the back loop—1 st inc'd.

MAKE 1 RIGHT (M1R)
Using left-hand needle, lift the bar between the stitch just worked and the next stitch from the back, knit this stitch through the front loop—1 st inc'd.

To construct this garment as a top-down raglan without sleeves, first work the back and front lace panels. After the raglan shaping is finished, join the back and front, cast on stitches for underarms, and continue working in the round to the bottom hem, which also contains a smidge of contrast color. Finally, stitches are picked up along the raglan seams and new stitches are cast on for shoulder straps.

A-line shaping, with negative ease in the bust and some positive ease in the waist and hips, is flattering on most body types. It also works well with plant-based fibers that may be prone to stretching in length due to weight.

Lace Panels (make 2)

Using CC and smaller needle, CO 33 (39, 45, 51, 57) sts.

Knit 4 rows.

Start working Lace Pattern chart. Rep Rows 1–24 of the pattern until you have 71 (81, 91, 103, 113) sts on needles after working 38 (42, 46, 52, 56) rows.

Place the first lace panel on stitch holder or scrap yarn and knit another panel in the same way.

lace pattern chart

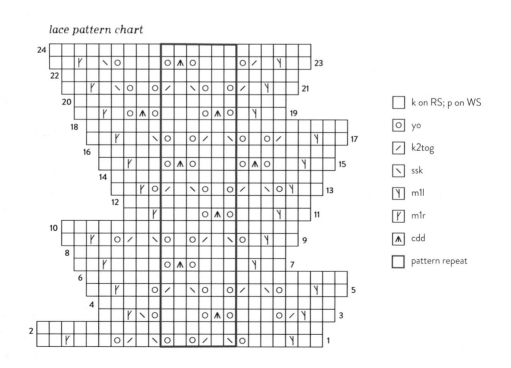

	k on RS; p on WS
○	yo
╱	k2tog
╲	ssk
Ⴘ	m1l
Ⴙ	m1r
⋀	cdd
	pattern repeat

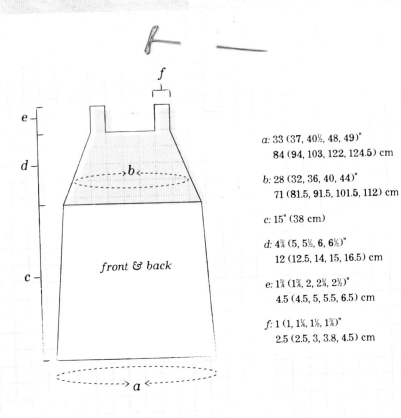

a: 33 (37, 40½, 48, 49)"
84 (94, 103, 122, 124.5) cm

b: 28 (32, 36, 40, 44)"
71 (81.5, 91.5, 101.5, 112) cm

c: 15" (38 cm)

d: 4¾ (5, 5½, 6, 6½)"
12 (12.5, 14, 15, 16.5) cm

e: 1¾ (1¾, 2, 2¼, 2½)"
4.5 (4.5, 5, 5.5, 6.5) cm

f: 1 (1, 1¼, 1½, 1¾)"
2.5 (2.5, 3, 3.8, 4.5) cm

Body

Place both lace panels on the same circular needle. Using MC and larger needles, knit across the first panel, pm, using the backward loop cast-on technique CO 6 (8, 8, 10, 12) sts, pm, knit across the second lace panel, pm, CO 3 (4, 4, 5, 6) sts, pm for BOR, CO 3 (4, 4, 5, 6) sts, pm. Join for knitting in the rnd—154 (178, 198, 226, 250) sts on needles.

Work in St st until piece measures 2" (5 cm) from underarm.

Inc rnd: (K to marker, sm, M1L, k to marker, M1R, sm) twice, k to end—4 sts inc'd.

Rep Inc rnd every 2" (5 cm) 5 times more (6 times total); 24 sts inc'd—178 (202, 222, 250, 274) sts.

Remove all markers except for BOR marker. Cont working in St st until piece measures 13½" (34.5 cm) from underarm.

Hem

Switch to smaller needle.

Rnd 1: Knit with CC.

Rnd 2: Purl with CC.

Rnd 3: Knit with MC.

Rnd 4: Purl with MC.

Repeat Rnds 1–4 three times more—16 rnds of hem total.

Knit 1 rnd with CC. BO purlwise with CC.

Shoulder straps

Start working in the middle of underarm cast-on sts. Using CC and smaller needles, pick up 1 st from every underarm cast-on st, pick up sts from the side of lace panel at a rate of 3 sts for every 4 rows. Using the backward loop cast-on technique, CO 20 (20, 22, 24, 28) sts. Pick up the same number of sts from the other lace panel and the rest of underarm sts. Pm for BOR. Work Garter stitch in the rnd (see Stitch Guide), starting with a purl rnd, for 1 (1, 1¼, 1½, 1¾)" (2.5 [2.5, 3, 3.8, 4.5] cm), ending with a knit rnd. BO all sts purlwise.

Finishing

Weave in ends and wet block to measurements.

VILLANDRY TUNIC

by holli yeoh

Clean geometric lines evoke the formal elegance
of a classical garden in this long, A-line tunic.
Only the simplest elements—stockinette,
reverse stockinette and garter-stitch borders,
slipped stitches, simple increases, and a little
short-row shaping at the shoulders—are
used, resulting in a design that is satisfyingly
minimalist, yet sophisticated.

finished size

Bust circumference: 32¾ (35½, 38¼, 41¾, 46, 50, 54¼, 57¾, 62, 66)" (83 [90, 97, 106, 117, 127, 138, 146.5, 157.5, 167.5] cm) using hanging gauge.

Intended to be worn with 1" (2.5 cm) ease using hanging gauge.

yarn

DK weight (#3 light).

Shown here: Shibui Knits Rain (100% cotton; 135 yd [123 m]/1¾ oz [50 g]): 2022 Mineral, 8 (8, 9, 10, 10, 12, 12, 13, 14, 15) skeins.

needles

Sizes U.S. 3, 4, and 6 (3.25, 3.5, and 4 mm): straight.

Size U.S. 3 (3.25 mm): 16" (40 cm) circular needle (cir).

Adjust needle size as necessary to obtain the correct gauge.

notions

Waste yarn for provisional CO; size U.S. G/6 (4 mm) crochet hook for provisional CO; stitch markers; tapestry needle.

gauge

21.5 sts and 32 rows = 4" (10 cm) in St st on size U.S. 6 (4 mm) needles, blocked.

22 sts and 30 rows = 4" (10 cm) in St st on size U.S. 6 (4 mm) needles, unblocked.

23 sts and 30 rows = 4" (10 cm) in St st on size U.S. 6 (4 mm) needles, blocked and hanging (see Notes).

notes

— Due to the inelastic nature of cotton and its tendency to stretch with wear, the finished dimensions are noted in the hanging gauge. The schematic dimensions and all calculations indicating a specified number of rows are noted in the blocked gauge. Any length measurements in the pattern refer to the unblocked gauge. Knit a sizable gauge swatch, recommended at least 6" (15 cm) wide, measure and record your gauge before and after blocking. Then hang the swatch fully supported along the top edge with blocking wire or several clothespins. Clip a skein of yarn across the bottom edge and let the swatch hang for a minimum of two days. Measure the swatch again. For your reference, the total body length of the sample grew about 2" (5 cm) after hanging.

— If your row gauges are vastly different from those in the pattern, multiply the length measurements by your unblocked gauge and divide by your blocked gauge to get the same dimensions as in the schematic. To determine how much your project will stretch while being worn, multiply the length measurements by your unblocked gauge and divide by your hanging gauge.

— The tunic is worked in pieces, top down, and seamed together.

Short rows are used to shape shoulders. Because the stitch pattern is reverse St st at the shoulders, I found German Short-rows to be the best method for this design.

stitch guide

CROSS PATTERN (worked over an even number of sts)

The Cross Pattern is comprised of 4 triangles. The top and bottom triangles are worked in reverse St st. The side triangles are worked in St st, except along the side slits where 3 edge sts on each side are worked in garter st with a slipped st selvedge.

The pattern instructions will guide you through this edging. All increases used to create the armhole and side shaping should be incorporated into the pattern and worked in St st.

Place marker in center with an equal number of sts on each side.

Upper row 1: (RS) K1, LT (see Techniques), purl to last 3 sts, RT (see Techniques), k1.

Upper row 2: (WS) P3, knit to last 3 sts, p3.

Upper row 3: K2, LT, purl to last 4 sts, RT, k2.

Upper row 4: P4, knit to last 4 sts, p4.

Upper row 5: K3, LT, purl to last 5 sts, RT, k3.

Upper row 6: P5, knit to last 5 sts, p5.

Upper row 7: K4, LT, purl to last 6 sts, RT, k4.

Upper row 8: P6, knit to last 6 sts, p6.

Cont in this manner, moving LT and RT 1 st over until they reach center marker, ending with a WS row.

Center cross row: (RS) Knit to 1 st before marker, RT (repositioning marker so it's still in the center), knit to end.

Lower row 1: Work to 2 sts before marker, RT, LT, work to end.

Lower row 2: Work to 1 st before marker, k2, work to end.

Lower row 3: Work to 3 sts before marker, RT, p2, LT, work to end.

Lower row 4: Work to 2 sts before marker, k4, work to end.

Lower row 5: Work to 4 sts before marker, RT, p4, LT, work to end.

Lower row 6: Work to 3 sts before marker, K6, work to end.

Lower row 7: Work to 5 sts before marker, RT, p6, LT, work to end.

Lower row 8: Work to 4 sts before marker, k8, work to end.

Cont in this manner, moving LT and RT 1 st over until they reach the last knit stitch worked before the selvedge, ending with a WS row.

Once cross is completed, work in reverse St st.

LEFT LIFTED INCREASE (LLI)

Use left needle to pick up st 2 rows directly below last st worked and knit into it—1 st inc'd

RIGHT LIFTED INCREASE (RLI)

With right needle, knit into right shoulder of st in row directly below the next st on left needle—1 st inc'd.

PROVISIONAL CROCHET CAST-ON

With waste yarn, make a slip knot and insert crochet hook. Holding hook in right hand and knitting needle in the left, *bring working yarn behind needle and with hook, reach over top of needle and crochet a chain st, thus wrapping yarn around needle; rep from * until desired number of sts are cast on. Work a few more chain sts (not around knitting needle) and fasten off.

note: I also like to use the Provisional Crochet Cast-On method for situations where I need to cast on additional sts at the end of a row, as follows: At end of row, hold needle with sts in left hand as if to work a new row. Slip first st onto crochet hook. With working yarn (not waste yarn) and using the Provisional Crochet Cast-On method, cast on desired number of sts, transfer last st from hook to needle. You're welcome to use your preferred method for casting on sts, but note that this method is specified in the instructions. If you substitute another method for the center front necklines, the marker needs to be moved over one st to the left.

Back

LEFT SHOULDER

Shoulder is shaped with short-rows. I suggest using the German Short-row method (see Techniques). Remember when working past a turn from an earlier row to work both strands of the double stitch together.

With size U.S. 6 (4 mm) needles, waste yarn, and Provisional Crochet Cast-On method, CO 7 (7, 7, 8, 10, 11, 13, 15, 16, 19) sts.

Row 1: (RS) Knit.

Short-rows 2 and 3: (WS) and (RS) P2, k1 (1, 1, 2, 3, 1, 2, 3, 2, 2), turn. Purl to last 2 sts, k2.

Sizes – (–, –, –, –, 50, 54¼, 57¾, 62, 66)" only
Short-rows 4 and 5: P2, k– (–, –, –, –, 5, 6, 8, 6, 7), turn. Purl to last 2 sts, k2.

Sizes – (–, –, –, –, –, –, –, 62, 66)" only
Short-rows 6 and 7: P2, k– (–, –, –, –, –, –, –, 10, 12), turn. Purl to last 2 sts, k2.

ALL SIZES–LEFT NECK SHAPING

Row 8: (WS) P2, knit to last 2 sts, p2.

Inc Row 9: (RS) K2, purl to last 4 sts, p1f&b twice, k2—9 (9, 9, 10, 12, 13, 15, 17, 18, 21) sts.

Row 10: Rep Row 8.

Row 11: K2, purl to last 2 sts, k2, using Provisional Crochet Cast-On method, CO 13 (13, 13, 13, 14, 14, 14, 15, 15) sts—22 (22, 22, 23, 25, 27, 29, 31, 33, 36) sts.

Row 12: Knit to last 2 sts, p2.

Break yarn and set Left Shoulder aside.

If using a circular needle, CO Right Shoulder onto other end of same needle.

RIGHT SHOULDER

With size U.S. 6 (4 mm) needles, waste yarn, and Provisional Crochet Cast-On method, CO 7 (7, 7, 8, 10, 11, 13, 15, 16, 19) sts.

Row 1: (WS) Knit.

Short-rows 2 and 3: (RS) and (WS) K2, p1 (1, 1, 2, 3, 1, 2, 3, 2, 2), turn. Knit to last 2 sts, p2.

Sizes – (–, –, –, –, 50, 54¼, 57¾, 62, 66)" only
Short-rows 4 and 5: K2, p– (–, –, –, –, 5, 6, 8, 6, 7), turn. Knit to last 2 sts, p2.

Sizes – (–, –, –, –, –, –, –, 62, 66)" only
Short-rows 6 and 7: K2, p– (–, –, –, –, –, –, –, 10, 12), turn. Knit to last 2 sts, p2.

ALL SIZES–RIGHT NECK SHAPING

Row 8: (RS) K2, purl to last 2 sts, k2.

Inc Row 9: (WS) P2, knit to last 4 sts, k1f&b twice, p2—9 (9, 9, 10, 12, 13, 15, 17, 18, 21) sts.

Row 10: Rep Row 8.

Row 11: P2, knit to last 2 sts, p2, using Provisional Crochet Cast-On method, CO 13 (13, 13, 13, 13, 14, 14, 14, 15, 15) sts—22 (22, 22, 23, 25, 27, 29, 31, 33, 36) sts.

Row 12: Purl to last 2 sts, k2.

Joining Row 13: (WS) P2, knit to end, using Provisional Crochet Cast-On method, CO 16 (16, 17, 17, 17, 17, 18, 18, 19, 19) sts, pm, CO 14 (14, 15, 15, 15, 15, 16, 16, 17, 17) sts, with WS facing knit across Left Shoulder to last 2 sts, p2—74 (74, 74, 76, 80, 86, 90, 94, 100, 106) sts; 15 (15, 16, 16, 16, 16, 17, 17, 18, 18) new neckline sts on each side of marker.

Next row: (RS) K2, purl to last 2 sts, k2.

Next row: P2, knit to last 2 sts, p2.

Rep last 2 rows 4 (4, 4, 4, 4, 3, 3, 3, 4, 4) times more.

BEGIN CROSS PATTERN

Read ahead before continuing. Cross Pattern is established after neckline shaping is completed and before armhole shaping begins. Cross Pattern is continued throughout the length of the Back and is worked concurrently with armhole shaping, side shaping, and the edging for the side slits.

Beg with Row 1, work 26 (22, 22, 18, 14, 12, 12, 8, 6, 4) rows of Cross Pattern.

ARMHOLE SHAPING

Single Inc row: (RS) K4, LLI, work in patt to last 4 sts, RLI, k4—2 sts inc'd.

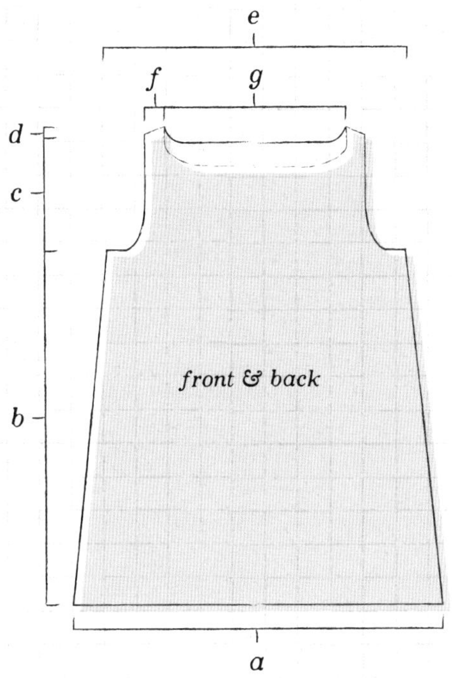

e

f   g

d

c

b

front & back

a

a: 22 (23½, 24½, 26¾, 28¼, 30½, 32¾, 35, 36¾, 39)"
56 (59.5, 62, 68, 72, 77.5, 83, 89, 93.5, 99) cm

b: 29¼ (30, 30½, 30¾, 31, 32¼, 32¾, 33¼, 33¾, 34¼)"
74.5 (76, 77.5, 78, 78.5, 82, 83, 84.5, 85.5, 87) cm

c: 7 (7¼, 7¼, 7½, 7¾, 8, 8¼, 8½, 9, 9¼)"
18 (18.5, 18.5, 19, 19.5, 20.5, 21, 21.5, 23, 23.5) cm

d: ½ (½, ½, ½, ½, ¾, ¾, ¾, 1, 1)"
1.3 (1.3, 1.3, 1.3, 1.3, 2, 2, 2, 2.5, 2.5) cm

e: 17¾ (19¼, 20¾, 22¾, 25, 27¼, 29½, 31¼, 33½, 35¾)"
45 (49, 52.5, 58, 63.5, 69, 75, 79.5, 85, 90.5) cm

f: 1¼ (1¼, 1¼, 1½, 1¾, 2, 2½, 2¾, 3, 3½)"
3 (3, 3, 3.8, 4.5, 5, 6.5, 7, 7.5, 9) cm

g: 11¼ (11¼, 11½, 11½, 11½, 12, 12¼, 12¼, 13, 13)"
28.5 (28.5, 29, 29, 29, 30.5, 31, 31, 33, 33) cm

Clean geometric lines evoke the formal elegance of a classical garden in this long, A-line tunic.

Working in patt, rep Single Inc row every RS row 4 (7, 7, 10, 12, 13, 14, 17, 19, 21) times more, ending with a WS row—84 (90, 90, 98, 106, 114, 120, 130, 136, 146) sts.

Sizes – (–, 38¼, 41¾, 46, 50, 54¼, 57¾, 62, 66)" only
Double Inc row: (RS) K4, LLI, k2, LLI, work in patt to last 6 sts, RLI, k2, RLI, k4—84 (90, 94, 102, 110, 118, 124, 134, 140, 150) sts. Work 1 WS row.

Sizes – (–, –, –, 46, 50, 54¼, 57¾, 62, 66)" only
Double Inc row: (RS) K4, LLI, k3, LLI, work in patt to last 7 sts, RLI, k3, RLI, k4—84 (90, 94, 102, 114, 122, 128, 138, 144, 154) sts. Work 1 WS row.

Sizes – (–, –, –, –, –, 54¼, 57¾, 62, 66)" only
Double Inc row: (RS) K4, LLI, k4, LLI, work in patt to last 8 sts, (RLI, k4) twice—84 (90, 94, 102, 114, 122, 132, 142, 148, 158) sts. Work 1 WS row.

Sizes – (–, –, –, –, –, –, –, 62, 66)" only
Double Inc row: (RS) K4, LLI, k5, LLI, work in patt to last 9 sts, (RLI, k5) twice—84 (90, 94, 102, 114, 122, 132, 142, 152, 162) sts. Work 1 WS row.

All Sizes
Working in patt, CO 6 (7, 9, 10, 10, 12, 13, 13, 14, 15) sts at the end of the next 2 rows—96 (104, 112, 122, 134, 146, 158, 168, 180, 192) sts.

Work even in patt until piece measures 2½ (2¾, 3½, 4¼, 5, 5, 5½, 6, 6¼, 6¾)" (6.5 [7, 9, 11, 12.5, 12.5, 14, 15, 16, 17] cm) from armhole CO, ending with a WS row.

SIDE SHAPING
Inc row: (RS) Work 4 sts, LLI, work in patt to last 4 sts, RLI, work 4 sts—2 sts inc'd.

Working in patt, rep Inc row every 12th (12th, 14th, 12th, 14th, 16th, 16th, 14th, 14th, 14th) row 5 (5, 4, 4, 3, 3, 3, 3, 3, 3) times more, ending with a WS row—108 (116, 122, 132, 142, 154, 166, 176, 188, 200) sts.

BEGIN SIDE SLIT
Next row: (RS) Sl 1 wyf, k2, work in patt to last 3 sts, k3. This row establishes garter st edging for side slits.

Rep last row while cont with Cross Pattern and Side Shaping every 12th (12th, 14th, 12th, 14th, 16th, 16th, 14th, 14th, 14th) row 5 (5, 5, 6, 5, 5, 5, 6, 5, 5) times more—118 (126, 132, 144, 152, 164, 176, 188, 198, 210) sts.

Work even until piece measures 22½ (23, 23½, 23¼, 23¼, 24½, 24½, 24¾, 25, 25)" (57 [58.5, 59.5, 59, 59, 62, 62, 63, 63.5, 63.5] cm) from underarm CO, ending with a WS row.

Change to size U.S. 4 (3.5 mm) needles.

Next row: (RS) Sl 1 wyf, knit to end.

Rep last row 5 times more. BO all sts.

Front
RIGHT SHOULDER
When casting on both shoulders, leave a tail of working yarn (not waste yarn) 13 (13, 13, 14, 16, 16, 18, 19, 20, 22)" (33 [33, 33, 36, 41, 41, 46, 49, 51, 56] cm) long to be used for three-needle BO.

With size U.S. 6 (4 mm) needles, waste yarn, and Provisional Crochet Cast-On method, CO 7 (7, 7, 8, 10, 11, 13, 15, 16, 19) sts.

Row 1: (RS) Knit.

Short-rows 2 and 3: (WS) and (RS) P2, k1 (1, 1, 2, 3, 1, 2, 3, 2, 2), turn. Purl to last 2 sts, k2.

Sizes – (–, –, –, –, 50, 54¼, 57¾, 62, 66)" only
Short-rows 4 and 5: P2, k– (–, –, –, –, 5, 6, 8, 6, 7), turn. Purl to last 2 sts, k2.

Sizes – (–, –, –, –, –, –, –, 62, 66)" only
Short-rows 6 and 7: P2, k– (–, –, –, –, –, –, –, 10, 12), turn. Purl to last 2 sts, k2.

ALL SIZES—RIGHT NECK SHAPING
Next row and all WS rows: P2, knit to last 2 sts, p2.

Single Inc row: (RS) K2, purl to last 3 sts, p1f&b, k2—1 st inc'd.

Rep Single Inc row every RS row 3 (3, 3, 3, 3, 0, 0, 0, 1, 1) time(s) more, ending with a WS row—11 (11, 11, 12, 14, 12, 14, 16, 18, 21) sts.

Double Inc row: (RS) K2, purl to last 4 sts, p1f&b twice, k2—2 sts inc'd.

Rep Double Inc row 1 (1, 1, 1, 1, 3, 3, 3, 3, 3) time(s) more, ending with a WS row—15 (15, 15, 16, 18, 20, 22, 24, 26, 29) sts.

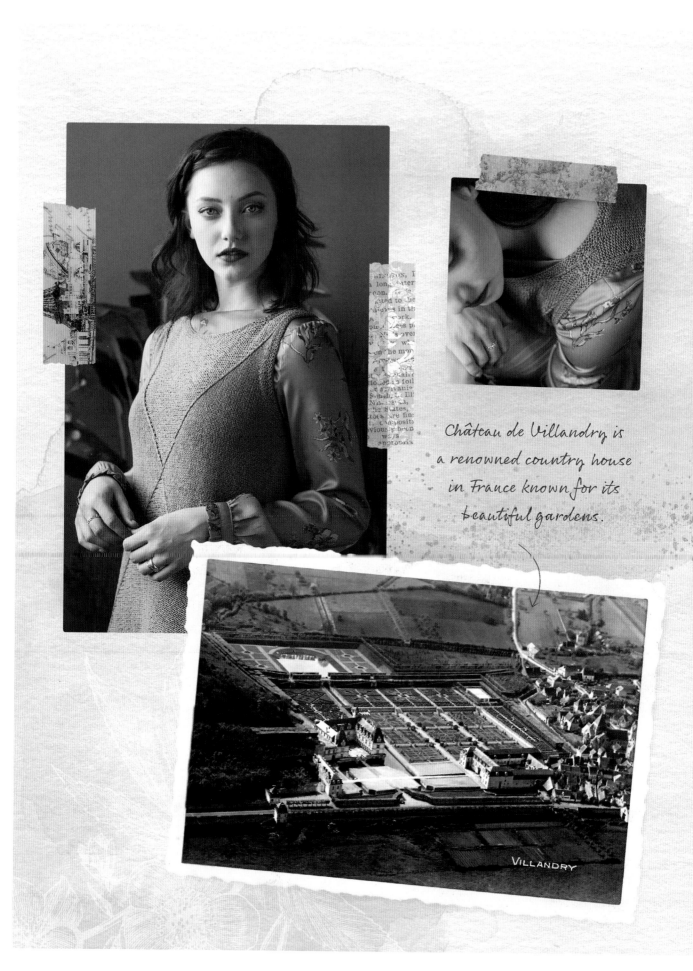

Château de Villandry is a renowned country house in France known for its beautiful gardens.

VILLANDRY

Next row: (RS) K2, purl to last 2 sts, k2, using Provisional Crochet Cast-On, CO 7 sts—22 (22, 22, 23, 25, 27, 29, 31, 33, 36) sts.

Next row: (WS) Knit to last 2 sts, p2.

Break yarn and set Right Shoulder aside.

If using a circular needle, cast on Left Shoulder onto other end of same needle.

LEFT SHOULDER

With size U.S. 6 (4 mm) needles, waste yarn, and Provisional Crochet Cast-On method, CO 7 (7, 7, 8, 10, 11, 13, 15, 16, 19) sts.

Row 1: (WS) Knit.

Short-rows 2 and 3: (RS) and (WS) K2, p1 (1, 1, 2, 3, 1, 2, 3, 2, 2), turn. Knit to last 2 sts, p2.

Sizes – (–, –, –, –, 50, 54¼, 57¾, 62, 66)″ only
Short-rows 4 and 5: K2, p– (–, –, –, –, 5, 6, 8, 6, 7), turn. Knit to last 2 sts, p2.

Sizes – (–, –, –, –, –, –, –, 62, 66)″ only
Short-rows 6 and 7: K2, p– (–, –, –, –, –, –, –, 10, 12), turn. Knit to last 2 sts, p2.

ALL SIZES LEFT NECK SHAPING
Next row and all RS rows: K2, purl to last 2 sts, k2.

Single Inc row: (WS) P2, knit to last 3 sts, k1f&b, p2—1 st inc'd.

Rep Single Inc row every WS row 3 (3, 3, 3, 3, 0, 0, 0, 1, 1) time(s) more, ending with a RS row—11 (11, 11, 12, 14, 12, 14, 16, 18, 21) sts.

Double Inc row: (WS) P2, knit to last 4 sts, k1f&b twice, p2—2 sts inc'd.

Rep Double Inc row 1 (1, 1, 1, 1, 3, 3, 3, 3, 3) time(s) more, ending with a RS row—15 (15, 15, 16, 18, 20, 22, 24, 26, 29) sts.

Next row: (WS) P2, knit to last 2 sts, p2, using Provisional Crochet Cast-On method, CO 7 sts—22 (22, 22, 23, 25, 27, 29, 31, 33, 36) sts.

Next row: (RS) Purl to last 2 sts, k2.

Joining row: (WS) P2, knit to end, CO 16 (16, 17, 17, 17, 17, 18, 18, 19, 19), pm, CO 14 (14, 15, 15, 15, 15, 16, 16, 17, 17), with WS facing knit across Right Shoulder to last 2 sts, p2—74 (74, 74, 76, 80, 86, 90, 94, 100, 106) sts; 15 (15, 16, 16, 16, 16, 17, 17, 18, 18) new neckline sts on each side of marker.

BEGIN CROSS PATTERN
Work as for Back from Begin Cross Pattern to end.

Finishing

Block pieces to schematic measurements. Remove provisional CO from shoulders and place sts on separate needles. Holding WS tog, with size U.S. 4 (3.5 mm) needle, join left shoulder seam using three-needle BO (see Techniques) worked tightly, working from armhole edge toward neck edge. Repeat for right shoulder, working pwise from armhole edge to neck edge. Using mattress st (see Techniques), sew side seams from side slit (identified by slipped st selvedge) opening to armhole.

NECKBAND
Using size U.S. 3 (3.25 mm) cir needle, with RS facing, pick up and knit 68 (68, 70, 70, 70, 74, 76, 76, 84, 84) sts evenly along Front neckline from left shoulder to right shoulder, then 68 (68, 70, 70, 70, 74, 76, 76, 84, 84) sts along Back neckline to left shoulder—136 (136, 140, 140, 140, 148, 152, 152, 168, 168) sts.

Place marker and join to work in the round.

Rnd 1: Purl.

Rnd 2: Knit.

Rep last 2 rnds once more. Rep Rnd 1 once. BO all sts.

ARMHOLE BANDS
Using size U.S. 3 (3.25 mm) cir needle, with RS facing, beg at side seam, pick up and knit 6 (7, 9, 10, 10, 12, 13, 13, 14, 15) sts along underarm BO, 37 (38, 39, 39, 40, 41, 43, 43, 46, 47) sts evenly along armhole edge to shoulder seam, 37 (38, 39, 39, 40, 41, 43, 43, 46, 47) sts to underarm BO, 6 (7, 9, 10, 10, 12, 13, 13, 14, 15) sts along underarm BO—86 (90, 96, 98, 100, 106, 112, 112, 120, 124) sts.

Work as for Neckband.

Repeat for other armhole.

lorate top

Lorate is a versatile summer top with an easy-
to-knit lace pattern at the back and a stockinette
stitch front. It was inspired by a desire to create
a versatile yet unique lace-pattern top that
can be worn for any occasion throughout the
warmer months of the year. Worked in a wool
and linen blend, this top can be worn alone
or paired with a cardigan on cooler days.

BY ANNIKA ANDREA WOLKE

finished size

Bust circumference: about 32 (34, 38, 42, 44)" (81 [86, 97, 107, 112] cm).

yarn

Fingering weight (#1 super fine).

Shown here: Blacker Yarns Lyonesse (50% Falkland wool, 50% linen; 190 yd [174 m]/ 1¾ oz [50g]): Quartz, 4 (4, 5, 6, 7) balls.

needles

Size U.S. 2 (2.75 mm).

Size U.S. 3 (3.25 mm).

Adjust needle size as necessary to obtain the correct gauge.

notions

2 stitch holders or waste yarn; tapestry needle.

gauge

23 sts and 32 rows = 4" (10 cm) in St st pattern on size U.S. 3 needles.

23 sts and 37.5 rows = 4" (10 cm) in lace pattern on size U.S. 3 needles.

notes

— When working the lace pattern at the sides only work decreases/increases when the corresponding increase/decrease can be worked. If that is not possible, work in St st.

— Before starting the front neck shaping, read the instructions to the end to make sure you know where to place Lorate chart B.

Back

Using smaller needles, CO 95 (105, 115, 129, 145) sts.

Row 1: K1, (p1, k1) to end.

Row 2: P1, (k1, p1) to end.

Rep last 2 rows 8 more times.

Change to larger needles. Starting with Row 1 of Lorate chart A and within the size markers of the size you are knitting, work in lace pattern until the back measures 14½ (15, 15¼, 15¾, 16¼)" (37 [38, 39, 40, 41] cm) from cast-on edge, ending with a RS facing for next row.

Armholes

Keeping lace pattern correct, shape armholes as folls:

Row 1: (RS) BO 4 (5, 6, 6, 8) sts, work in patt from chart as set to end—91 (100, 109, 123, 137) sts.

Row 2: BO 4 (5, 6, 6, 8) sts, work in patt from chart as set to end—87 (95, 103, 117, 129) sts.

Row 3: K1, sl 1, k1, psso, work in patt from chart as set to last 3 sts, k2tog, k1—2 sts dec'd.

Row 4: P1, p2tog, purl to last 3 sts, p2tog tbl, p1—2 sts dec'd.

Rep Rows 3 and 4 a further 2 (2, 2, 5, 5) times—75 (83, 91, 93, 105) sts.

Next row: (RS) K1, sl 1, k1, psso, work in patt from chart as set to last 3 sts, k2tog, k1—2 sts dec'd.

Next row: Purl.

Rep the last 2 rows 3 (1, 4, 3, 3) more time(s)—67 (79, 81, 85, 97) sts.

Size – (34, –, –, –)" only

Next row: (RS) K1, sl 1, k1, psso, work in patt from chart as set to last 3 sts, k2tog, k1—2 sts dec'd.

Next row: Purl.

Next row: Work in patt as set.

Next row: Purl.

Rep last 4 rows – (1, –, –, –) time – – (75, –, –, –) sts.

All Sizes

Cont working in patt from chart as set until armhole meas 6¾ (7, 7½, 7¾, 8¼)" (17 [18, 19, 19.5, 21] cm), ending with a RS facing for next row.

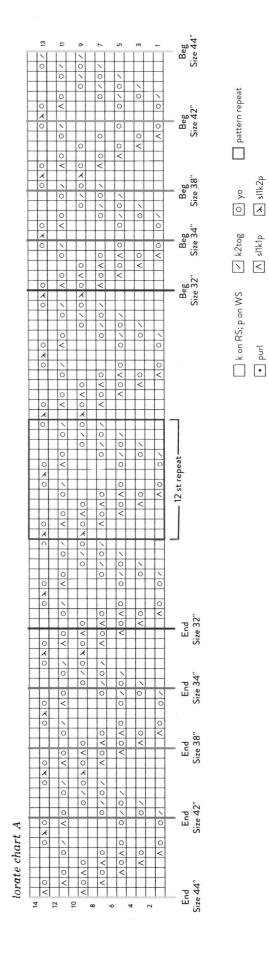

lorate chart A

pattern repeat

yo · sl1k2p

k2tog · sl1k1p

k on RS; p on WS

· purl

Shoulder & Back Neck Shaping

Keeping lace pattern correct, shape shoulders and back neck as folls:

Row 1: (RS) BO 2 (2, 3, 4, 4) sts, work in patt from chart as set across 16 (17, 19, 20, 24) sts. Turn work.

Work sides separately.

RIGHT SHOULDER

Row 2: P1, p2tog, purl to end—1 st dec'd.

Row 3: BO 2 (2, 3, 3, 4) sts, work in patt as set to last 3 sts, k2tog, k1—12 (13, 14, 15, 18) sts.

Row 4: Rep Row 2.

Row 5: BO 2 (3, 3, 3, 4) sts, work in patt as set to last 3 sts, k2tog, k1—8 (8, 9, 10, 12) sts.

Row 6: Rep Row 2.

Row 7: BO 3 (3, 3, 4, 5) sts, work in patt as set to last 3 sts, k2tog, k1.

Row 8: Purl.

Row 9: BO rem 3 (3, 4, 4, 5) sts.

Place center 31 (37, 37, 37, 41) sts on holder.

LEFT SHOULDER

With RS facing, rejoin yarn to remaining sts.

Row 1: (RS) Work across all sts in patt as set.

Row 2: BO 2 (2, 3, 4, 4) sts, work in patt as set to end—16 (17, 19, 20, 24) sts.

Row 3: K1, sl 1, k1, psso, work in patt as set to end—1 st dec'd.

Row 4: BO 2 (2, 3, 3, 4) sts, work in patt as set to last 3 sts, p2tog tbl, p1—12 (13, 14, 15, 18) sts.

Row 5: Rep Row 3.

Row 6: BO 2 (3, 3, 3, 4) sts, work in patt as set to last 3 sts, p2tog tbl, p1—8 (8, 9, 10, 12) sts.

Row 7: Rep Row 3.

Row 8: BO 3 (3, 3, 4, 5) sts, work in patt as set to last 3 sts, p2tog tbl, p1.

Row 9: Work in patt as set.

Row 10: BO rem 3 (3, 4, 4, 5) sts.

Front

Work Front as given for Back but working in St st after the rib until the armhole measures 3¼ (3¾, 4, 4, 4¼)" (8.5 [9.5, 10, 10, 11] cm), ending with a RS facing for next row.

LEFT FRONT NECK & SHOULDER

Row 1: (RS) Work in patt for 24 (28, 30, 35, 38) sts, turn work.

Row 2: P1, p2tog, purl to end—1 st dec'd.

Row 3: Work in patt to 3 sts, k2tog, k1—1 st dec'd.

Rep last 2 rows 4 (5, 5, 5, 5) more times—14 (16, 18, 23, 26) sts.

Next row: Purl.

Next row: Work in patt to last 3 sts, k2tog, k1—1 st dec'd.

Rep last 2 rows 1 (2, 1, 1, 2) more time(s)—12 (13, 16, 21, 23) sts.

Sizes – (–, –, 42, 44)" only

Work 3 rows in patt.

Next row: (RS) Work in patt to last 3 sts, k2tog, k1— – (–, –, 20, 22) sts.

All Sizes

And AT THE SAME TIME on Row 16 (18, 18, 18, 18) of neck shaping (which is a RS row), work Row 1 from Lorate chart B within your size markers instead of St st. Cont working from chart, completing shaping where applicable, until you have worked the 14 rows of the chart once.

Cont working in lace patt as set where possible, shaping shoulders as folls:

Row 1: (RS) BO 2 (2, 3, 4, 4) sts, work in patt as set to end.

Row 2: Purl.

Row 3: BO 2 (2, 3, 4, 4) sts, work in patt as set to end.

Row 4: Rep Row 2.

lorate chart B

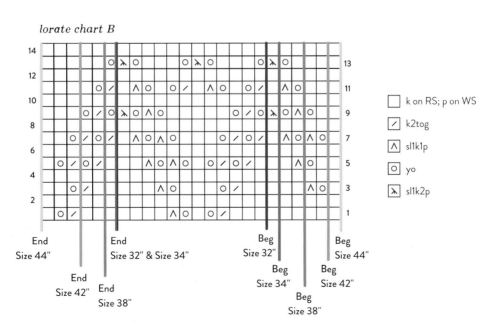

Legend:

☐	k on RS; p on WS
╱	k2tog
∧	sl1k1p
○	yo
⅄	sl1k2p

End Size 44"
End Size 42"
End Size 38"
End Size 32" & Size 34"
Beg Size 32"
Beg Size 34"
Beg Size 38"
Beg Size 42"
Beg Size 44"

Lorate implies "strap"; the decorative straps of this tee hit just the right note between form and function.

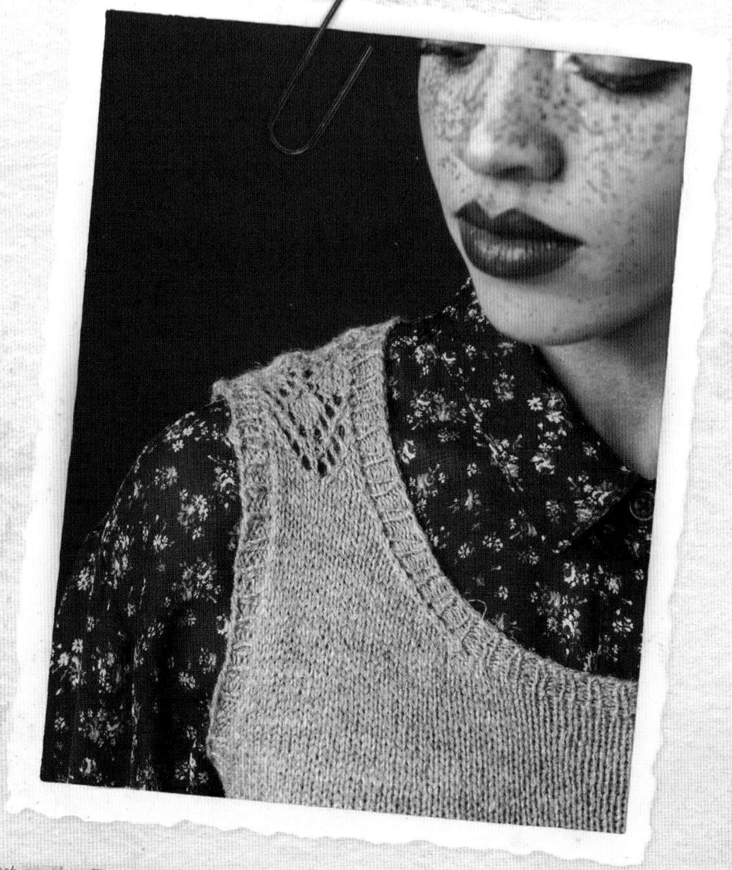

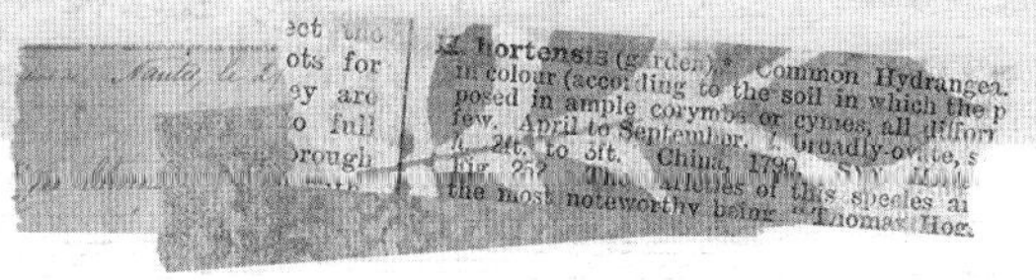

lorate chart C

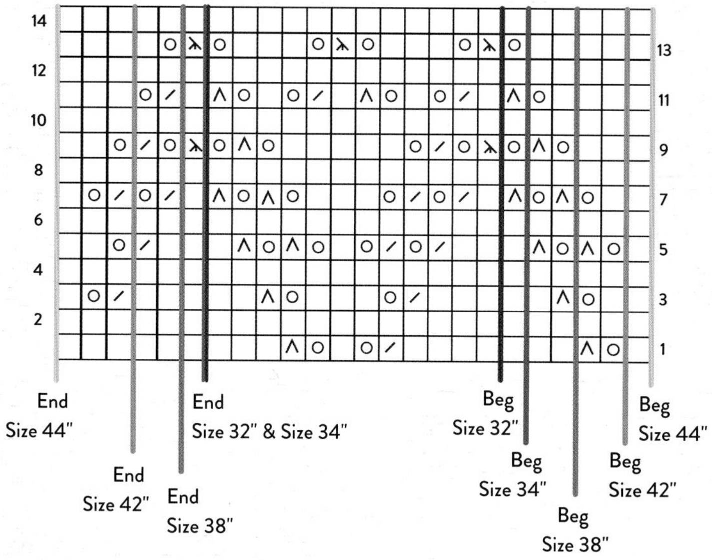

14
13
12
11
10
9
8
7
6
5
4
3
2
1
End Size 44"
End Size 42"
End Size 38"
End Size 32" & Size 34"
Beg Size 32"
Beg Size 34"
Beg Size 38"
Beg Size 42"
Beg Size 44"

- ☐ k on RS; p on WS
- ⁄ k2tog
- Λ sl1k1p
- O yo
- ⋋ sl1k2p

Row 5: BO 2 (3, 3, 4, 4) sts, work in patt as set to end.

Row 6: Rep Row 2.

Row 7: BO 3 (3, 3, 4, 5) sts, work in patt as set to end.

Row 8: Purl.

Row 9: BO rem 3 (3, 4, 4, 5) sts.

Place center 19 (19, 21, 21, 21) sts on holder.

RIGHT FRONT NECK & SHOULDER

With RS facing, rejoin yarn to remaining sts.

Row 1: (RS) Work across all sts in patt as set.

Row 2: Purl to last 3 sts, p2tog tbl, p1—1 st dec'd.

Row 3: K1, sl 1, k1, psso, work in patt to end—1 st dec'd.

Rep last 2 rows 4 (5, 5, 5, 5) more times—14 (16, 18, 23, 26) sts.

Next row: Purl.

Next row: K1, sl 1, k1, psso, work in patt to end—1 st dec'd.

Rep last 2 rows 1 (2, 1, 1, 2) more time(s)—12 (13, 16, 21, 23) sts.

Sizes – (–, –, 42, 44)" only

Work 3 rows in patt.

Next row: (RS) K1, sl 1, k1, psso, work in patt to end— – (–, –, 20, 22) sts.

All Sizes

And AT THE SAME TIME, on Row 16 (18, 18, 18, 18) of neck shaping (which is a RS row), work Row 1 from Lorate chart C within your size markers instead of St st. Cont working from chart, completing shaping where applicable, until you have worked the 14 rows of the chart once.

Cont working in lace patt as set where possible, shaping shoulders as folls:

Row 1: (RS) Work in patt as set.

Row 2: BO 2 (2, 3, 4, 4) sts, work in patt as set to end.

Row 3: Work in patt as set.

Row 4: BO 2 (2, 3, 4, 4) sts, work in patt as set to end.

Row 5: Rep Row 3.

Row 6: BO 2 (2, 3, 4, 4) sts, work in patt as set to end.

Row 7: Rep Row 3.

Row 8: BO 3 (3, 3, 4, 5) sts, work in patt as set to end.

Row 9: Work in patt as set.

Row 10: BO rem 3 (3, 4, 4, 5) sts.

Finishing

Weave in ends and block pieces to measurements. Sew side seams and shoulder seams.

NECKBAND

Starting at back and using smaller needles, pick up and knit 31 (37, 37, 37, 41) sts from holder, 8 (8, 8, 8, 8) sts from left back neck, 24 (26, 28, 30, 30) sts from left front neck, 19 (19, 21, 21, 21) sts from holder at front, 24 (26, 28, 30, 30) sts from right front neck, 8 (8, 8, 8, 8) sts from right back neck—114 (124, 130, 134, 138) sts. Join to work in the rnd.

Rnd 1: *K1, p1; rep from * to end.

Rep last rnd 5 more times. BO all sts in patt.

ARMHOLES

Starting at side seam and using smaller needles, pick up and knit 88 (96, 104, 112, 120) sts. Join to work in the rnd.

Rnd 1: *K1, p1; rep from * to end.

Rep last rnd 3 more times.

BO all sts in patt. Rep on other armhole.

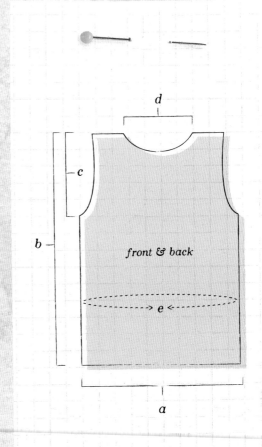

a: 16¼ (18, 19¾, 22, 24¾)"
(41.5 [45.5, 50, 56, 63] cm)

b: 21¼ (22, 22¾, 23½, 24½)"
(54 [56, 58, 59.5, 62] cm)

c: 6¾ (7, 7½, 7¾, 8¼)"
(17 [18, 19, 19.5, 21] cm)

d: 5¼ (6¼, 6¼, 6¼, 7)"
(13.5 [16, 16, 16, 18] cm)

e: 33 (36½, 40, 45, 50½)"
(84 [92.5, 101.5, 114.3, 128.3] cm)

A delicate, leafy lace adds softness
and intrigue to this shell.

SEABROOK TOP

The Seabrook Top is named for a lovely
barrier island off the coast of Charleston,
South Carolina. This picturesque spot makes
a perfect backdrop for summer evening
strolls, and wearing this pullover is the
perfect complement to seaside walks. The
linen yarn combined with the exaggerated
lace keeps the wearer from overheating.

by kirsten singer-joel

finished size

Bust circumference: 41 (44, 47, 50, 54, 60, 63)" (104 [112, 119.5, 127, 137, 152.5, 160] cm).

Designed to be worn with approximately 10" (25.5 cm) positive ease.

yarn

DK weight (#3 light).

Shown here: Erika Knight Studio Linen (100% cellulose—linen/flax; 131 yd [120 m]/ 1¾ oz [50 g]): #406 Lacy, 8 (8, 9, 9, 10, 10, 11) skeins.

needles

Size U.S. 5 (3.75 mm).

Adjust needle size as necessary to obtain the correct gauge.

notions

Stitch markers; scrap yarn; tapestry needles.

gauge

20 sts and 32 rows = 4" (10 cm) in St st on size U.S. 5 needles.

Back

CO 102 (110, 118, 126, 134, 150, 158) sts.

Knit 4 rows.

Begin working in St st until piece measures 15½ (15½, 16¼, 16¼, 16¼, 16½, 17)" (39.5 [39.5, 41.5, 41.5, 41.5, 42, 43] cm) from cast-on, ending with a WS row.

ARMHOLE SHAPING

Inc row: (RS) K2, M1, knit to last 2 sts, M1, k2—2 sts inc'd.

Work Inc row 4 (4, 4, 5, 5, 5, 7) more times—112 (120, 128, 138, 146, 162, 174) sts.

CO 10 (12, 12, 14, 14, 16, 16) sts at beg of next 2 rows—132 (144, 152, 166, 174, 194, 206) sts. Work even until piece measures 5 (5½, 6, 6½, 7, 7½, 8)" (12.5 [14, 15, 16.5, 18, 19, 20.5] cm), ending with a WS row.

NECK SHAPING

Knit 48 (52, 56, 60, 64, 68, 72) sts, join 2nd ball of yarn, BO center 36 (40, 40, 46, 46, 58, 62) sts, knit to end—48 (52, 56, 60, 64, 68, 72) sts for each shoulder.

> *note: Work right and left shoulders at the same time with 2 different balls of yarn.*

Next row: (WS) (Left side of neck) Purl; (Right side of neck) Purl.

Next row: (RS) (Right side of neck) Knit to last 3 sts, k2tog, k1; (Left side of neck) K1, skp, knit to end—1 st dec'd at neck edge each side.

Next row: (WS) (Left side of neck) Purl; (Right side of neck) Purl.

Rep these 2 rows once more—46 (50, 54, 58, 62, 66, 70) sts.

BO all sts.

Front

CO 102 (110, 118, 126, 134, 150, 158) sts.

Knit 4 rows.

Begin working Wide Lace Pattern:

Row 1: (RS) K5, *k2tog, 2yo, ssk, k4; rep from * 11 (13, 14, 15, 16, 18, 19) more times, k1.

Row 2: (WS) K1, purl across to last st, k1. Work 2yo as p1, k1.

Work Rows 1 and 2 six more times.

Next row: (RS) K5, *k2tog, 2yo, ssk, k4; rep from * 10 (12, 13, 14, 15, 17, 18) more times, knit to end.

Cont as established, working the pattern repeat one less time every 14th row until piece measures 15½ (15½, 16¼, 16¼, 16¼, 16½, 17)" (39.5 [39.5, 41.5, 41.5, 41.5, 42, 43] cm) from CO, ending with a WS row.

ARMHOLE SHAPING

Inc Row: (RS) K2, M1, knit to last 2 sts, M1, k2—2 sts inc'd.

Work Inc Row 4 (4, 4, 5, 5, 5, 7) more times—112 (120, 128, 138, 146, 162, 174) sts.

CO 10 (12, 12, 14, 14, 16, 16) sts at beg of next 2 rows—132 (144, 152, 166, 174, 194, 206) sts.

Cont as established until piece measures 3 (3½, 4, 4½, 5, 5½, 6)" (7.5 [9, 10, 11.5, 12.5, 14, 15] cm), ending with a WS row.

NECK SHAPING

Knit 51 (55, 60, 64, 69, 73, 78) sts, join 2nd ball of yarn, BO center 30 (34, 32, 38, 36, 48, 50) sts, knit to end—51 (55, 60, 64, 69, 73, 78) sts for each shoulder.

> *note: Work right and left shoulders at the same time from 2 different balls of yarn.*

Next row: (WS) (Right side of neck) Purl; (Left side of neck) Purl.

Next row: (RS) (Left side of neck) Knit to last 3 sts, k2tog, k1; (Right side of neck) K1, skp, knit to end—1 st dec'd at neck edge each side.

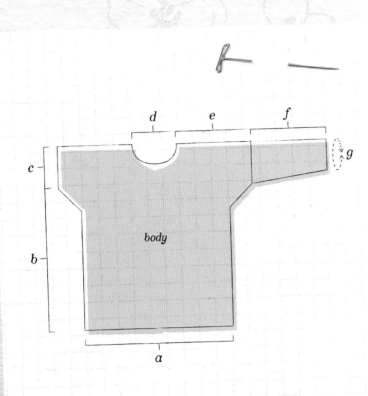

a: 20½ (22, 24, 25, 27, 28, 30)"
52 (56, 61, 63.5, 68.5, 71, 76) cm

b: 15½ (15½, 16¼, 16¼, 16¼, 16½, 17)"
39.5 (39.5, 41.5, 41.5, 41.5, 42, 43) cm

c: 5½ (6, 6½, 7, 7½, 8, 8½)"
14 (15, 16.5, 18, 19, 20.5, 21.5) cm

d: 6 (6¾, 6½, 7½, 7¼, 9½, 10)"
15 (17, 16.5, 19, 18.5, 24, 25.5) cm

e: 10¼ (11, 12, 12¾, 13¾, 14½, 15½)"
26 (28, 30.5, 32.5, 35, 37, 39.5) cm

f: 10 (10, 10, 10½, 11, 11½, 11½)"
25.5 (25.5, 25.5, 26.5, 28, 29, 29) cm

g: 9 (10, 11, 12, 13, 14, 15)"
23 (25.5, 28, 30.5, 33, 35.5, 38) cm

The longer length allows it to be worn as a cover-up for those who love the beach.

Next row: (WS) (Right side of neck) Purl; (Left side of neck) Purl.

Rep these 2 rows 4 (4, 5, 5, 6, 6, 7) more times—46 (50, 54, 58, 62, 66, 70) sts.

BO all sts.

Sleeves

Starting at armhole cast-on with RS of work facing, pick up and knit 55 (60, 65, 70, 75, 80, 85) sts. Work even in St st until pieces measures 2½ (2½, 2½, 3, 3, 3½, 3½)" (6.5 [6.5, 6.5, 7.5, 7.5, 9, 9] cm) from pick-up edge, ending with a WS row.

Dec row: (RS) K1, skp, knit to last 3 sts, k2tog, k1—2 sts dec'd.

Work Dec row every 8 rows 4 more times—45 (50, 55, 60, 65, 70, 75) sts.

Continue to work even until sleeve measures 10 (10, 10, 10½, 11, 11½, 11½)" (25.5 [25.5, 25.5, 26.5, 28, 29, 29] cm) from pick-up edge, ending with a RS row.

Knit 3 rows.

BO all sts.

Finishing

Block to measurements and weave in ends. Seam shoulders, sleeves, and sides using your preferred method.

Neckband

With RS facing and starting at left shoulder, pick up and knit 2 sts for every 3 rows worked along left front neck shaping, 1 st for every stitch bound off along front neck, 2 sts for every 3 rows along right front and back neck shaping, 1 st for every stitch bound off along back neck, 2 sts for every 3 rows along left back neck shaping. Pm and join for working in the rnd.

Rnd 1: Purl.

Rnd 2: Knit.

Rnd 3: Purl.

BO all sts.

kenno top

BY JOANNA IGNATIUS

Kenno means honeycomb in Finnish, making it an appropriate name for this merino-cotton top. The sweater is worked from the bottom up, starting with honeycomb lace—a lateral braid that separates the lace from the stockinette body. The front and back are worked separately from the armholes upward; then the neckline and armholes are finished with a sleek bind-off. Wear the Kenno Top alone or as a layering piece when the weather turns chillier.

finished size

About 34 (36, 38, 40, 42, 44)" (86.5 [91.5, 96.5, 101.5, 106.5, 112] cm) at bust, meant to be worn with approximately 2" (5 cm) of positive ease.

yarn

DK weight (#3 light).

Shown here: The Plucky Knitter Crew (75% merino wool, 25% cotton; 300 yd [274 m]/ 4 oz [113 g]): Dirty Blonde, 3 (3, 4, 4, 5) hanks.

needles

Size U.S. 6 (4 mm) circular (circ).

Size U.S. 4 (3 mm) circ for lateral braid.

Adjust needle size if necessary to obtain the correct gauge.

notions

4 stitch markers; size U.S. G/6 (4 mm) crochet hook; waste yarn or stitch holders; an extra needle for 3-needle bind-off; tapestry needle for weaving in ends.

gauge

24 sts and 29 rows = 4" (10 cm) in St st on size U.S. 6 (4 mm) needles.

notes

— The lateral braid tends to be stretchy and the yarnovers can be big, so go down a needle size if necessary. Make sure you work the yarnovers on the next round twisted.

Hem

With larger needles, CO 212 (228, 244, 260, 276, 296) sts and join in the round.

Rnd 1: K105 (113, 121, 129, 137, 145), pm, k1, pm, k105 (113, 121, 129, 137, 147), pm, k1, pm (BOR).

Rnd 2: Purl.

Rnd 3: Knit.

Rep the last two rnds once more, then work Rnd 2 once.

HONEYCOMB LACE

Set-up rnd: Work Honeycomb Lace chart, working the patt rep 12 (13, 14, 15, 18, 17) times, sm, p1, sm, working the patt rep 12 (13, 14, 15, 18, 17) times, sm, p1, sm (BOR).

Work in patt, repeating Rnds 1–16 three times, then work Rnd 17 once. Piece measures 6" (15 cm) from beg.

BRAID

Rnd 1: With smaller needles, yo, k2tog-tbl, *slip stitch back to LH needle, yo, k2tog-tbl; rep from * to end. Insert crochet hook from WS under the first lateral st and pull the last st from LH needle under it and place it back to RH needle.

Rnd 2: With larger needles, k to end (the yo's will be twisted).

Body

Shape with short-rows as folls:

Short-row 1: K to m, sm, k1, sm, k to m, sm, k1, sm, k5, turn.

Short-row 2: P to m, sm, p1, sm, p to m, sm, p1, sm, p5, turn.

Short-row 3: K to 4 sts before previous turn, turn (there are 4 sts between the turns).

Short-row 4: P to 4 sts before previous turn, turn.

Rep the last two rows once more.

Knit to BOR, working the double sts as one st. Knit one rnd, working the double sts as one st.

Continue working in St st until the Body measures 14½ (13½, 12½, 11½, 10½, 9½)" (37 [31.5, 32, 29, 26.5, 24] cm) measured from the side seam.

Dec rnd: K2tog, k to 2 sts before m, ssk, sm, k1, sm, k2tog, k to 2 sts before m, ssk, sm, k1, sm.

Work Dec rnd 1 (2, 3, 4, 5, 6) more time(s) every 1" (2.5 cm)—204 (216, 228, 240, 252, 268) sts. Work in St st for ½" (1.3 cm).

honeycomb lace chart

	knit
•	purl
∕	k2tog
∖	ssk
o	yo
⋀	cdd: sl2, k1, p2sso
	pattern repeat

Front

BO 5 (6, 7, 8, 9, 10) sts at BOR, k to m, rm, k1, rm. Turn, BO 5 (6, 7, 8, 9, 10) sts at beg of row, p to end—92 (96, 100, 104, 108, 114) sts.

Row 1: (RS) Ssk, k to 2 sts before end, k2tog.

Row 2: (WS) Sl 1 wyf, p1, psso, p to 2 sts before end, p2tog.

Repeat these two rows once more—84 (88, 92, 96, 100, 106) sts.

Continue to decrease on both ends only on every RS row 5 (5, 6, 7, 8, 9) times—74 (78, 80, 82, 84, 88) sts.

Continue to work in St st until armholes measure 2 (2½, 2½, 2½, 3, 3)" (5 [6.5, 6.5, 6.5, 7.5, 7.5] cm), ending with WS row.

LEFT FRONT

Row 1: (RS) K25 (27, 28, 29, 30, 32), k24 and place these 24 sts on a holder, BO 4 (4, 5, 5, 5, 6) sts, k to end.

Rows 2, 4, and 6: (WS) Purl.

Row 3: (RS) BO 2 sts, k to end.

Row 5: (RS) Ssk, k to end.

Rep the last two rows once more—15 (17, 17, 18, 19, 20) sts. Work in St st until armhole measures 7 (7½, 7½, 8, 8, 8½)" (18 [19, 19, 20.5, 20.5, 21.5] cm), ending with RS row.

Shape with short-rows as folls:

Short-row 1: (RS) K to 5 (6, 6, 6, 7, 8) sts before end, turn.

Rows 2 and 4: (WS) Purl.

Short-row 3: (RS) K to 3 sts before previous turn, turn.

Row 5: (RS) K to end, knitting the double sts as one st.

Break yarn and place the sts on a holder.

RIGHT FRONT

Join yarn at the neck opening edge.

Row 1: (WS) BO 4 (4, 5, 5, 5, 6) sts, p to end.

Rows 2, 4, and 6: (RS) Knit.

Row 3: (WS) BO 2 sts, p to end.

Row 5: (WS) Sl 1, p1, psso, p to end.

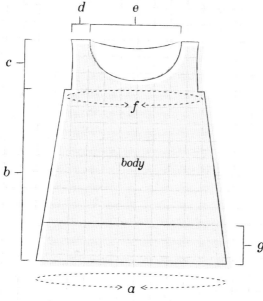

a: 34¾ (37½, 40¼, 42¾, 45¼, 48½)"
88.5 (95, 102, 108.5, 115, 123) cm

b: 16" (40.5 cm)

c: 7 (7½, 7½, 8, 8, 8½)"
18 (19, 19, 20.5, 20.5, 21.5) cm

d: 2½ (2¾, 2¾, 3, 3¼, 3¼)"
6.5 (7, 7, 7.5, 8.5, 8.5) cm

e: 7¼ (7¼, 7½, 7½, 7½, 8)"
18.5 (18.5, 19, 19, 19, 20.5) cm

f: 34 (36, 38, 40, 42, 44)"
86.5 (91.5, 96.5, 101.5, 106.5, 112) cm

g: 6"(15 cm)

Rep the last two rows once more—15 (17, 17, 18, 19, 20) sts. Work in St st until armhole measures 7 (7½, 7½, 8, 8, 8½)" (18 [19, 19, 20.5, 20.5, 21.5] cm).

Shape with short-rows as folls:

Short-row 1: (WS) P to 5 (6, 6, 6, 7, 8) sts before end, turn.

Rows 2 and 4: (RS) Knit.

Short-row 3: (RS) P to 3 sts before previous turn, turn.

Row 5: (RS) P to end, purling the double sts as one st.

Break yarn and place the sts on a holder.

Back

Rejoin yarn on RS.

BO 5 (6, 7, 8, 9, 10) sts, k to m, rm, k1. Turn, BO 5 (6, 7, 8, 9, 10) sts at beg of row, p to end—92 (96, 100, 104, 108, 114) sts.

Row 1: (RS) Ssk, k to 2 sts before end, k2tog.

Row 2: (WS) Sl 1 wyf, p1, psso, p to 2 sts before end, p2tog.

Repeat these two rows once more—84 (88, 92, 96, 100, 106) sts.

Continue to decrease on both ends only on every RS row 5 (5, 6, 7, 8, 9) times—74 (70, 80, 82, 84, 88) sts.

Continue to work in St st until armholes measure 7 (7½, 7½, 8, 8, 8½)" (18 [19, 19, 20.5, 20.5, 21.5] cm).

SHOULDERS AND NECK

You can either keep the 44 (44, 46, 46, 46, 48) neck sts alive on the needles or place them on a holder.

Right Shoulder

Shape with short-rows as folls:

With RS facing, k15 (17, 17, 18, 19, 20), turn.

Short-row 1: (WS) P to 5 (6, 6, 6, 7, 8) sts before end, turn.

Rows 2 and 4: (RS) Knit.

Short-row 3: (WS) P to 3 sts before previous turn, turn.

Row 5: (WS) P to end, purling the double sts as one st.

Turn the top inside out, place the Front Shoulder sts on an extra needle and with RS facing, BO shoulder sts using 3-needle BO (see Techniques). Break yarn.

Left Shoulder

Shape with short-rows as folls:

With WS facing, join yarn at other end of back piece, p15 (17, 17, 18, 19, 20), turn.

Short-row 1: (RS) K to 5 (6, 6, 6, 7, 8) sts before end, turn.

Rows 2 and 4: (WS) Purl.

Short-row 3: (RS) K to 3 sts before previous turn, turn.

Row 5: (RS) K to end, knitting the double sts as one st.

Turn the top inside out, place the Front Shoulder sts on an extra needle and with RS facing, BO shoulder sts using 3-needle BO. Break yarn.

Finishing

NECKLINE

Beg at Right Shoulder seam, pick up and knit 5 sts along Right Back Shoulder, 44 (44, 46, 46, 46, 48) sts from Back neck, 5 sts along Left Back Shoulder, 26 (26, 26, 26, 26, 27) sts along Left Front, 24 sts from Front neck, 26 (26, 26, 26, 26, 27) sts along Right Front. Purl one rnd—130 (130, 132, 132, 132, 136) sts.

K1, do not drop from LH needle, k this st and the following st tog tbl, *sl 2 sts back to LH needle, k1, k2tog tbl; rep from * to end until you have 2 sts left on RH needle. BO remaining sts, sew ends of edging together.

ARMHOLES

Beg at underarm, pick up and knit 100 (100, 104, 108, 110, 112) sts around the armhole. Purl one round. BO as Neckline.

Block to measurements and weave in ends.

LACE LEAF TEE

Who says you can't knit a yoke-style
sweater for spring? Just substitute lace for
colorwork and use a cotton/silk blend, and
you have a wearable sweater throughout
most seasons. Yoke increases are worked
into the lace and traveling stitch patterning.

by amy gunderson

finished size
Bust circumference: About 32¾ (37, 42¼, 47¼, 53, 58¼)" (83 [94, 108, 120, 134.5, 148] cm)

yarn
DK weight (#3 light).

Shown here: Fibra Natura Papyrus (78% cotton, 22% silk); 131 yd [120 m]/1¾ oz [50 g]): #229-04 Dogwood, 9 (10, 11, 12, 14, 15) balls.

needles
Size U.S. 5 (3.75 mm): 16 and 32" (40 and 80 cm) circular (cir), set of double-pointed (dpn).

Adjust needle size if necessary to obtain the correct gauge.

notions
Markers (m); cable needle (cn); stitch holders; tapestry needle.

gauge
22 sts and 29 rows = 4" (10 cm) in St st.

notes
This sweater is knit seamlessly from the top down. Short-rows are worked after the charted yoke pattern in order to raise the back neck without disrupting the patterning.

stitch guide

RIGHT TWIST (RT)
K2tog but do not slip sts from needle, knit the first st again, slip both sts from needle.

LEFT TWIST (LT)
Knit the second st on the left needle through the back loop, knit the first st through the front loop, slip both sts from needle.

1x1x1 LEFT CROSS (LC)
Sl first st to cn and hold in front, RT from left needle, k1 from cn.

Neck

With shorter cir needle, CO 108 (108, 112, 116, 120, 122) sts. Pm and join to work in the rnd, being careful not to twist. Beg of rnd falls at Back Neck.

Purl 1 rnd, knit 1 rnd, purl 1 rnd.

Sizes 32¾ (37, 42¼, –, –, –)" only
Inc rnd: *K27 (6, 4, –, –, –), M1; rep from * 3 (17, 27, –, –, –) more times—4 (18, 28, –, –, –) sts inc'd, 112 (126, 140, –, –, –) sts.

Size – (–, –, 47¼, –, –)" only
Inc rnd: *K3, M1; rep from * 37 more times, k2—38 sts inc'd, 154 sts.

Size 53" only
*K3, M1, k2, M1; rep from * 23 more times —48 sts inc'd, 168 sts.

Size 58¼" only
*K2, M1; rep from * 59 more times, k2—60 sts inc'd, 182 sts.

All Sizes
Work Rnds 1–14 of Yoke chart. Patt will be repeated 16 (18, 20, 22, 24, 26) times across rnd.

Rnd 15: Sl last st from Rnd 14 back to left needle, complete Rnd 15 as shown.

Work Rnds 16–21 of Yoke chart.

Rnd 22: Remove BOR m, sl last st from Rnd 21 back to left needle, complete Rnd 22 as shown to last st, k1, replacing m in original spot between first and second sts of first 1×1×1 LC of rnd.

Work Rnds 23–30 of Yoke chart.

Rnd 31: Remove beg-of-rnd m, sl last st from Rnd 30 back to left needle, complete Rnd 31 as shown to last st, k1, replacing m in original spot between first and second sts of first 1×1×1 LC of rnd.

Work Rnds 32–45 of chart—288 (324, 360, 396, 432, 468) sts.

Knit 1 rnd.

Shape Back with short-rows as folls:

Short-row 1: (RS) K32 (38, 44, 51, 58, 65), w&t.

Short-row 2: (WS) P64 (76, 88, 102, 116, 130), w&t.

yoke chart

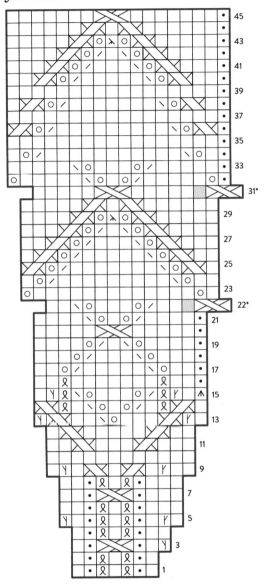

☐ knit	⅄ m1R
• purl	▨ no stitch
⅄ k1tbl	⤫ 1×1×1 LC (see Stitch Guide)
╱ k2tog	⤬ LT (see Stitch Guide)
╲ ssk	⤬ RT (see Stitch Guide)
○ yo	* Work as indicated in instructions
⅄ sl1k2p	☐ pattern repeat
⋀ cdd: sl2, k1, p2sso	

Short-row 3: Knit to wrapped st, work st tog with wrap, k4, w&t.

Short-row 4: Purl to wrapped st, work st tog with wrap, p4, w&t.

Short-rows 5–8: Rep Rows 3 and 4 twice.

Next rnd: Knit to end, working tog wraps with their sts.

Work even in St st if necessary until piece measures 7¼ (7¾, 8¼, 8¾, 9¼, 9½)" (18.5 [19.5, 21, 22, 23.5, 24] cm) from CO edge. Measure straight down front neck.

DIVIDE BODY & SLEEVES
Rnd 1: K42 (48, 54, 61, 68, 75) Right Back sts, place next 60 (66, 72, 76, 80, 84) sts on holder for Right Sleeve, CO 3 (3, 4, 4, 5, 5) sts, pm for side, CO 3 (3, 4, 4, 5, 5) sts, k84 (96, 108, 122, 136, 150) Front sts, place next 60 (66, 72, 76, 80, 84) sts on holder for Left Sleeve, CO 3 (3, 4, 4, 5, 5) sts, pm for side, CO 3 (3, 4, 4, 5, 5) sts, knit across rem 42 (48, 54, 61, 68, 75) Left Back sts—180 (204, 232, 260, 292, 320) sts rem for Body.

Work even in St st for 2" (5 cm).

SHAPE WAIST
Inc rnd: *Knit to 1 st before side m, M1R, k1, sm, k1, M1L; rep from *1 more time, knit to end—4 sts inc'd, 184 (208, 236, 264, 296, 324) sts.

Rep Inc rnd every 12 (12, 0, 10, 0, 10) rnds 2 (2, 0, 2, 0, 2) more times, then rep Inc rnd every 14 (14, 16, 12, 16, 12) rnds 3 (3, 4, 4, 4, 4) times—204 (228, 252, 288, 312, 348) sts. Remove side ms. Work even in St st until piece meas 13½" (34.5 cm) from underarm.

HEM
Work Rnds 1 and 2 of Hem chart.

Rnd 3: Remove BOR m, sl last st from Rnd 2 back to left needle, complete Rnd 3 as shown to last st, k1, replacing m in original spot between first and second sts of first 1×1×1 LC of rnd.

Work Rnds 1–12 of Hem chart.

[Knit 1 rnd, purl 1 rnd] 2 times, knit 1 rnd.

Turn, BO all sts using 3-st I-Cord method (see Techniques) from WS.

hem chart

11

9

7

5

3*

1

12 st repeat

	knit
•	purl
	k1tbl
╱	k2tog
╲	ssk
O	yo
	sl1k2p
⋀	cdd: sl2, k1, p2sso
	no stitch
	1×1×1 LC (see Stitch Guide)
	LT (see Stitch Guide)
	RT (see Stitch Guide
*	work as indicated in instructions
	pattern repeat

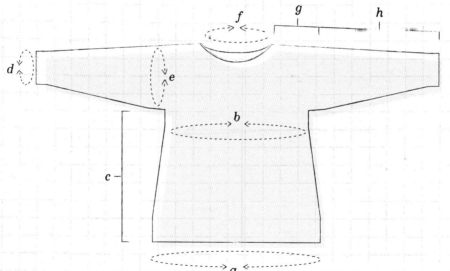

a: 37 (41½, 45¾, 52¼, 56¾, 63¼)"
94 (105.5, 116, 132.5, 144, 160.5) cm

b: 32¾ (37, 42¼, 47¼, 53, 58¼)"
83 (94, 107.5, 120, 134.5, 148) cm

c: 16½" (42 cm)

d: 8 (8, 8¼, 8¼, 8¾, 8¾)"
20.5 (20.5, 21, 21, 22, 22) cm

e: 12 (13, 14½, 15¼, 16¼, 17)"
30.5 (33, 37, 38.5, 41.5, 43) cm

f: 19¾ (19¾, 20¼, 21, 21¾, 22¼)"
50 (50, 51.5, 53.5, 55, 56.5) cm

g: 7¼ (7¾, 8¼, 8¾, 9¼, 9½)"
18.5 (19.5, 21, 22, 23.5, 24) cm

h: 16½" (42 cm)

Though the name of this tee evokes Spring, it's versatile enough to be worn year-round. Style it to your liking!

Sleeves

Return held sts to dpns.

Rnd 1: Beg at center of underarm, pick up and knit 3 (3, 4, 4, 5, 5) sts, knit across held sts, pick up and knit 3 (3, 4, 4, 5, 5) sts along other side of underarm—66 (72, 80, 84, 90, 94) sts.

Work even in St st for 3" (7.5 cm).

Dec rnd: K1, k2tog, knit to last 3 sts, ssk, k1—2 sts dec'd, 64 (70, 78, 82, 88, 92) sts rem.

Rep Dec rnd every 10 (8, 6, 6, 6, 6) rnds 5 (7, 15, 11, 7, 3) more times, then rep Dec rnd every 8 (6, 4, 4, 4, 4) rnds 5 (6, 1, 7, 13, 19) time(s)—44 (44, 46, 46, 48, 48) sts rem.

Work even in St st until Sleeve meas 15¾" (40 cm) from underarm.

[Purl 1 rnd, knit 1 rnd] 2 times.

Turn, BO all sts using 3-st I-Cord method from WS.

Finishing
NECK EDGING

With shorter cir needle, pick up and knit 108 (108, 112, 116, 120, 122) sts.

Turn, BO all sts using 3-st I-Cord method from WS.

Sew ends of I-Cord tog. Weave in ends and block.

driftwood vest

Weathered and warmed by the sun
and water, driftwood takes shape
organically—captured here perfectly in
the Driftwood Vest. In alternating bands of
lace, this vest is revealed as a decorative-
yet-functional wardrobe staple that, like its
namesake, suggests waves and motion.

BY KIRSTEN SINGER-JOEL

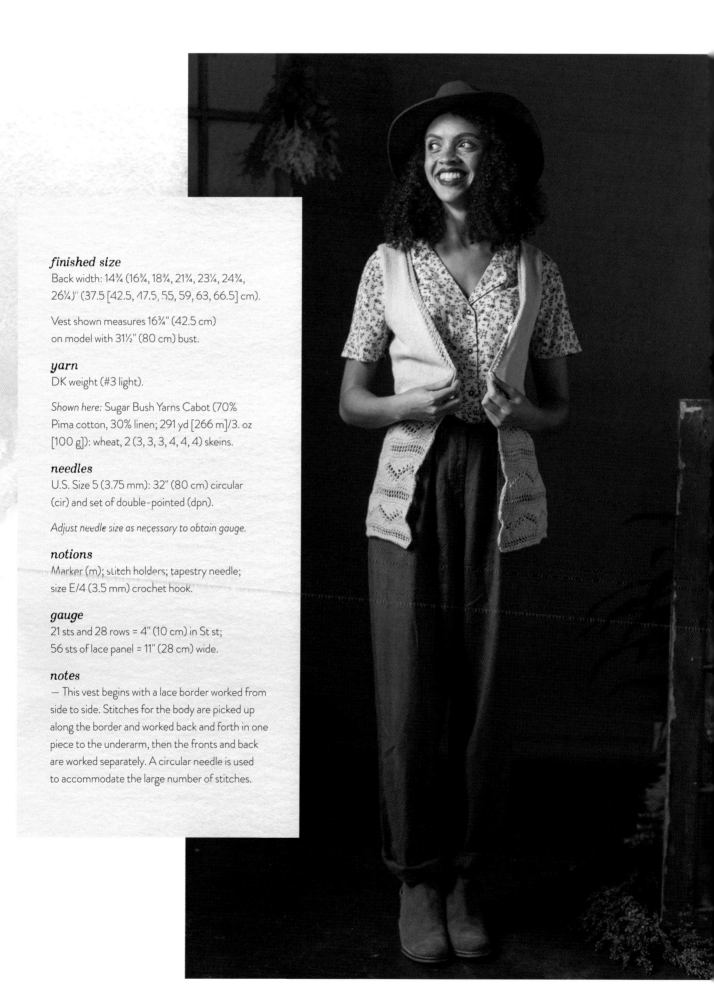

finished size
Back width: 14¾ (16¾, 18¾, 21¼, 23¼, 24¾, 26¼)" (37.5 [42.5, 47.5, 55, 59, 63, 66.5] cm).

Vest shown measures 16¾" (42.5 cm) on model with 31½" (80 cm) bust.

yarn
DK weight (#3 light).

Shown here: Sugar Bush Yarns Cabot (70% Pima cotton, 30% linen; 291 yd [266 m]/3. oz [100 g]): wheat, 2 (3, 3, 3, 4, 4, 4) skeins.

needles
U.S. Size 5 (3.75 mm): 32" (80 cm) circular (cir) and set of double-pointed (dpn).

Adjust needle size as necessary to obtain gauge.

notions
Marker (m); stitch holders; tapestry needle; size E/4 (3.5 mm) crochet hook.

gauge
21 sts and 28 rows = 4" (10 cm) in St st; 56 sts of lace panel = 11" (28 cm) wide.

notes
— This vest begins with a lace border worked from side to side. Stitches for the body are picked up along the border and worked back and forth in one piece to the underarm, then the fronts and back are worked separately. A circular needle is used to accommodate the large number of stitches.

Body

BORDER

With cir needle, CO 56 sts. Do not join.

Work Lace chart for 29¼ (33¼, 37¼, 43, 45¾, 48¾, 51¾)" (74.5 [84.5, 94.5, 109, 116, 124, 131.5] cm), ending with a WS row.

BO all sts.

UPPER BODY

With cir needle and RS facing, pick up and knit 154 (174, 196, 226, 240, 256, 272) sts evenly spaced along one long edge of border. Do not join.

Next row: (WS) K3, yo, k2tog, purl to last 5 sts, k2, yo, k2tog, k1.

Next row: (RS) K3, yo, k2tog, knit to last 3 sts, yo, k2tog, k1. Cont in patt until piece measures 6 (6, 7, 7, 8, 8, 8)" (15 [15, 18, 18, 20.5, 20.5, 20.5] cm) from pick-up row, ending with a WS row.

DIVIDE FOR FRONTS & BACK

Next row: (RS) Work 5 sts in patt, ssk, k28 (33, 39, 45, 48, 52, 56), place these 34 (39, 45, 51, 54, 58, 62) sts on holder for right front, BO 6 (6, 6, 8, 8, 8, 8) sts, k72 (82, 92, 106, 114, 122, 130) and place these sts on holder for back, BO 6 (6, 6, 8, 8, 8, 8) sts, knit to last 7 sts, k2tog, work to end—34 (39, 45, 51, 54, 58, 62) sts rem for left front.

Left Front

Work 1 WS row.

SHAPE ARMHOLE & NECK

note: *Armhole and neck shaping occur simultaneously; read the foll section all the way through before proceeding.*

Next row: (RS) BO 2 (3, 3, 4, 4, 4, 5) sts, work to end.

Work 1 WS row.

lace chart

16-st rep

- ☐ k on RS; p on WS
- • k on WS
- ○ yo
- ⟋ k2tog on RS
- ⟍ ssk
- ⟍• k2tog on WS
- ☐ pattern repeat

Armhole dec row: (RS) K1, ssk, work to end—1 st dec'd.

Rep Armhole dec row every RS row 2 (2, 3, 3, 3, 5, 6) more times.

AT THE SAME TIME, shape neck as foll:

Neck dec row: (RS) Work to last 7 sts, k2tog, work to end—1 st dec'd.

Rep Neck dec row every RS row 2 (7, 15, 21, 24, 24, 24) more times, then every 4th row 10 (8, 5, 3, 2, 3, 3) times—16 (17, 17, 18, 19, 20, 22) sts rem when all shaping is complete.

Work even until armhole measures 7½ (8, 8½, 9, 9½, 10, 10)" (19 [20.5, 21.5, 23, 24, 25.5, 25.5] cm), ending with a WS row.

BO all sts.

Right Front

Return 34 (39, 45, 51, 54, 58, 62) held right front sts to needle and, with WS facing, rejoin yarn.

SHAPE ARMHOLE & NECK

{ *note:* Armhole and neck shaping occur simultaneously, read the foll section all the way through before proceeding.

Next row: (WS) BO 2 (3, 3, 4, 4, 4, 5) sts, work to end—32 (36, 42, 47, 50, 54, 57) sts rem.

Armhole dec row: (RS) Work to last 3 sts, k2tog, k1—1 st dec'd.

Rep Armhole dec row every RS row 2 (2, 3, 3, 3, 5, 6) more times.

AT THE SAME TIME, shape neck as foll:

Neck dec row: (RS) Work 5 sts, ssk, work to end—1 st dec'd.

Rep Neck dec row every RS row 2 (7, 15, 21, 24, 24, 24) more times, then every 4th row 10 (8, 5, 3, 2, 3, 3) times—16 (17, 17, 18, 19, 20, 22) sts rem when all shaping is complete.

Work even until armhole measures 7½ (8, 8½, 9, 9½, 10, 10)" (19 [20.5, 21.5, 23, 24, 25.5, 25.5] cm), ending with a WS row.

BO all sts.

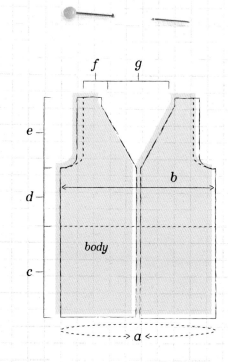

a: 29¼ (33¼, 37¼, 43, 45¾, 48¾, 51¾)" (74.5 [84.5, 94.5, 109, 116, 124, 131.5] cm)

b: 14¾ (16¾, 18¾, 21¾, 23¼, 24¾, 26¼)" (37.5 [42.5, 47.5, 55, 59, 63, 66.5] cm)

c: 11" (28 cm)

d: 6 (6, 7, 7, 8, 8, 8)" (15 [15, 18, 18, 20.5, 20.5, 20.5] cm)

e: 7½ (8, 8½, 9, 9½, 10, 10)" (19 [20.5, 21.5, 23, 24, 25.5, 25.5] cm)

f: 2¾ (3, 3, 3¼, 3½, 3½, 4)" (7 [7.5, 7.5, 8.5, 9, 9, 10] cm)

g: 5¼ (6, 7¼, 8¾, 9¼, 9½, 10)" (13.5 [15, 18.5, 22, 23.5, 24, 25.5] cm)

... as the driftwood burning
Learned its jewelled blaze
From the sea's blue splendor
Of colored nights and days.

— Sara Teasdale, excerpt
from Driftwood

BACK

Return 72 (82, 92, 106, 114, 122, 130) held back sts to needle and, with WS facing, rejoin yarn.

SHAPE ARMHOLES

BO 2 (3, 3, 4, 4, 4, 5) sts at beg of next 2 rows—68 (76, 86, 98, 106, 114, 120) sts rem.

Work 1 WS row.

Dec row: (RS) K1, ssk, knit to last 3 sts, k2tog, k1—2 sts dec'd.

Rep Dec row every RS row 4 (5, 6, 8, 10, 12, 12) more times—58 (64, 72, 80, 84, 88, 94) sts rem.

Work even until armhole measures 7 (7½, 8, 8½, 9, 9½, 9½)" (18 [19, 20.5, 21.5, 23, 24, 24] cm), ending with a WS row.

SHAPE NECK

Next row: (RS) K17 (18, 18, 19, 20, 21, 23) and place these sts on holder for right shoulder, BO 24 (28, 36, 42, 44, 46, 48) sts, knit to end—17 (18, 18, 19, 20, 21, 23) sts rem for left shoulder.

LEFT SHOULDER

Work 1 WS row even.

Dec row: (RS) K1, ssk, knit to end—1 st dec'd.

Rep Dec row every RS row once more—15 (16, 16, 17, 18, 19, 21) sts rem.

Work even until armhole measures 7½ (8, 8½, 9, 9½, 10, 10)" 19 [20.5, 21.5, 23, 24, 25.5, 25.5] cm), ending with a WS row.

BO all sts.

RIGHT SHOULDER

Return 17 (18, 18, 19, 20, 21, 23) held right shoulder sts to needle and, with WS facing, rejoin yarn.

Work 1 WS row even.

Dec row: (RS) Knit to last 3 sts, k2tog, k1—1 st dec'd.

Rep Dec row every RS row once more—15 (16, 16, 17, 18, 19, 21) sts rem.

Work even until armhole measures 7½ (8, 8½, 9, 9½, 10, 10)" (19 [20.5, 21.5, 23, 24, 25.5, 25.5] cm), ending with a WS row.

BO all sts.

Finishing

Weave in ends. Block to measurements.

Sew shoulder seams.

ARMHOLE EDGING

With dpn and RS facing, beg at center of underarm, pick up and knit 42 (45, 48, 51, 53, 56, 56) sts along armhole edge to shoulder seam, 42 (45, 48, 51, 53, 56, 56) sts along armhole edge to center of underarm—84 (90, 96, 102, 106, 112, 112) sts total.

Place marker and join in the rnd.

Purl 1 rnd.

BO all sts kwise.

BACK NECK EDGING

With crochet hook and RS facing, beg at right shoulder, work 4 sc along shaped edge of back neck, working below BO edge, sl st in each st along BO edge, work 4 sc along shaped edge to left shoulder.

Fasten off.

PUCK'S TUNIC

Puck's Tunic is a subtle, airy tee that toes the line between playful and sophisticated. It's perfect for staying cool on warm days, and the whimisical zigzag lace pattern on the front and back of this knitted top makes it unique. The tunic is made in two simple rectangles and seamed so that all the focus stays on that fanciful detailing.

by susanna IC

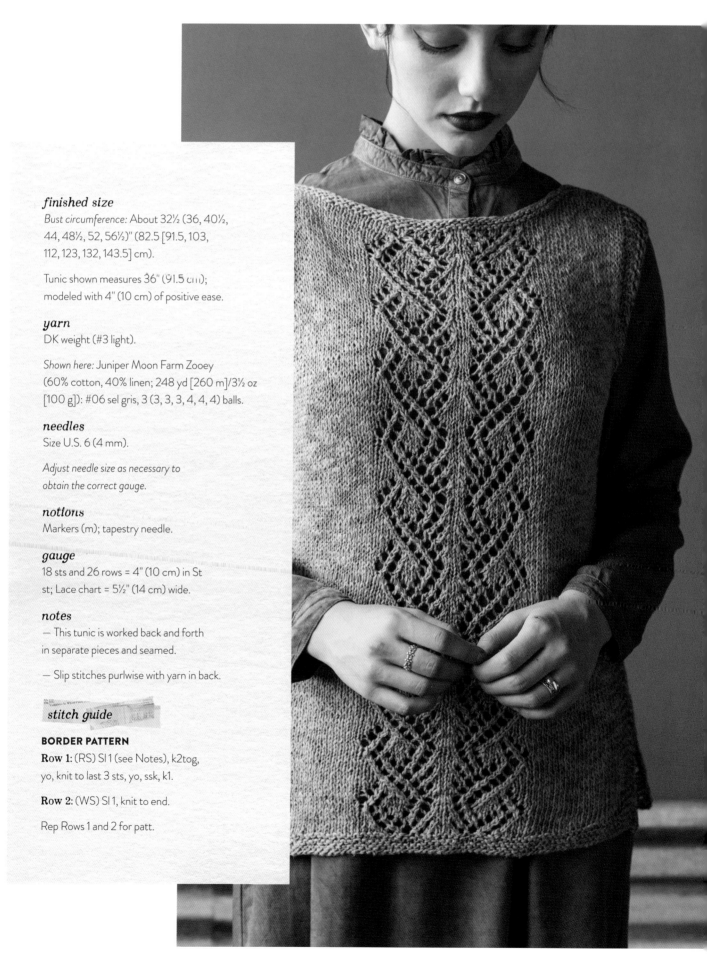

finished size

Bust circumference: About 32½ (36, 40½, 44, 48½, 52, 56½)" (82.5 [91.5, 103, 112, 123, 132, 143.5] cm).

Tunic shown measures 36" (91.5 cm); modeled with 4" (10 cm) of positive ease.

yarn

DK weight (#3 light).

Shown here: Juniper Moon Farm Zooey (60% cotton, 40% linen; 248 yd [260 m]/3½ oz [100 g]): #06 sel gris, 3 (3, 3, 3, 4, 4, 4) balls.

needles

Size U.S. 6 (4 mm).

Adjust needle size as necessary to obtain the correct gauge.

notions

Markers (m); tapestry needle.

gauge

18 sts and 26 rows = 4" (10 cm) in St st; Lace chart = 5½" (14 cm) wide.

notes

— This tunic is worked back and forth in separate pieces and seamed.

— Slip stitches purlwise with yarn in back.

stitch guide

BORDER PATTERN

Row 1: (RS) Sl 1 (see Notes), k2tog, yo, knit to last 3 sts, yo, ssk, k1.

Row 2: (WS) Sl 1, knit to end.

Rep Rows 1 and 2 for patt.

Front

CO 71 (79, 89, 97, 107, 115, 125) sts. Work Border patt (see Stitch Guide) for 6 rows, ending with a WS row.

Next row: (RS) Sl 1, k2tog, yo, k21 (25, 30, 34, 39, 43, 48), place marker (pm), work Lace chart over 23 sts, pm, k21 (25, 30, 34, 39, 43, 48), yo, ssk, k1.

Next row: (WS) Sl 1, k6, purl to last 7 sts, k7. Cont in patt as established until piece measures 23½ (23½, 24, 24, 24½, 24½, 25)" (59.5 [59.5, 61, 61, 62, 62, 63.5] cm) from CO, ending with a WS row.

Work Border patt for 4 rows.

BO all sts.

Back

Work as for front.

Finishing

Weave in ends.

Block pieces to measurements.

Sew 3 (3½, 4½, 5, 6, 6½, 7½)" (7.5 [9, 11.5, 12.5, 15, 16.5, 19] cm) shoulder seams. Sew side seams starting 8 (8, 8½, 8½, 9, 9, 9½)" (20.5, [20.5, 21.5, 21.5, 23, 23, 24] cm) from shoulder seam, leaving 5" (12.5 cm) vents at bottom.

lace chart

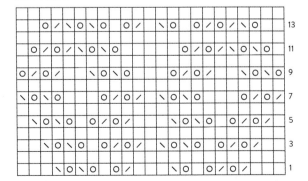

23 sts

☐ k on RS; p on WS

╱ k2tog

╲ ssk

○ yo

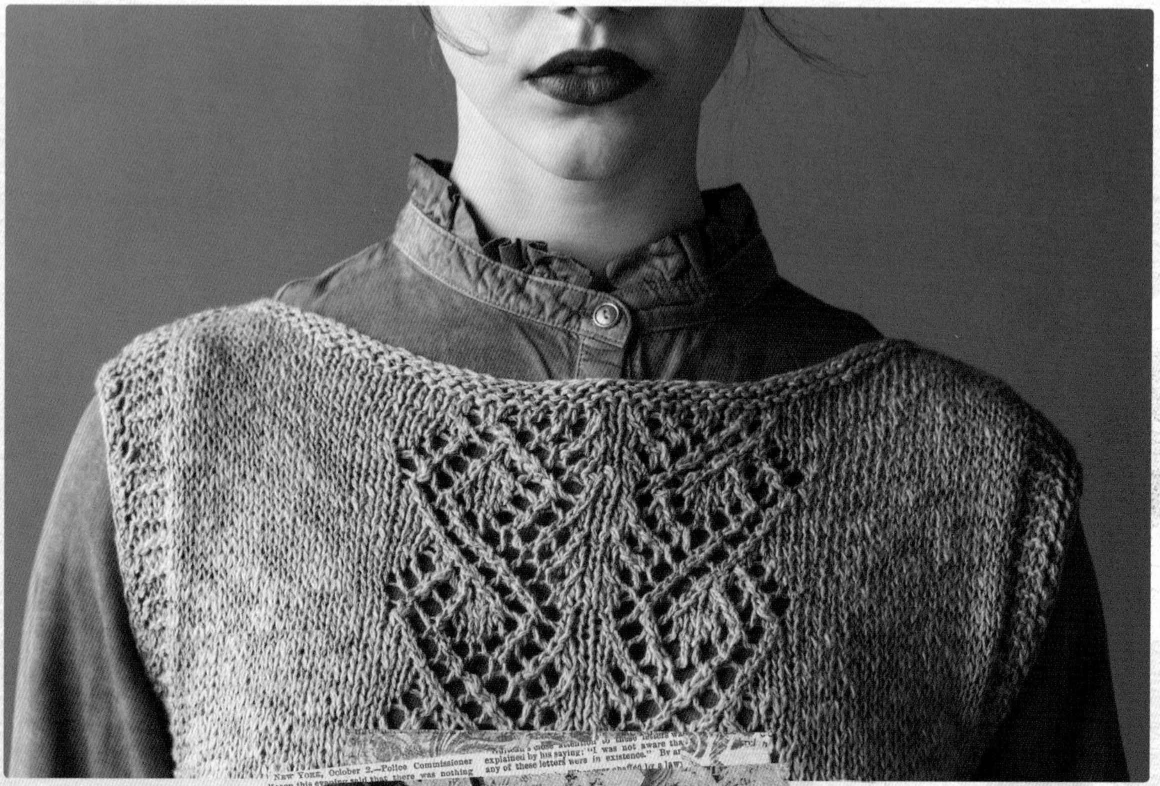

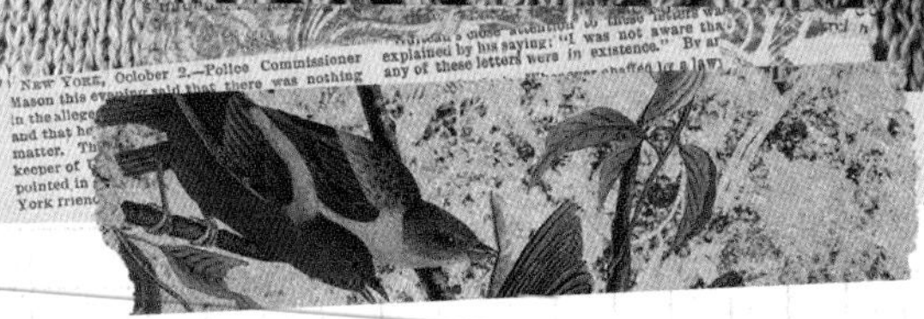

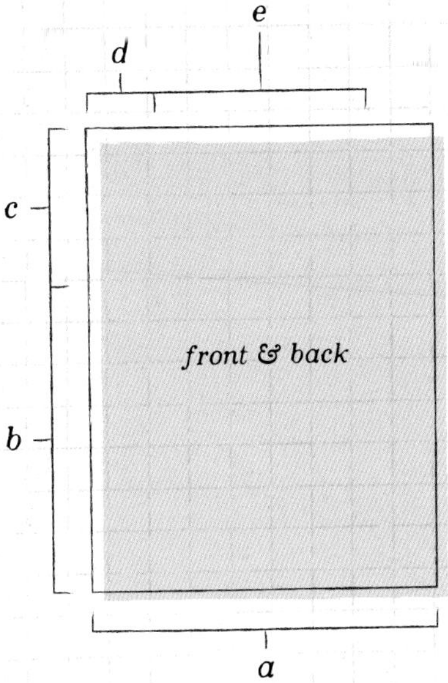

a: 16¼ (18, 20¼, 22, 24¼, 26, 28¼)"
(41.5 [45.5, 51.5, 56, 61.5, 66, 72] cm)

b: 15½" (39.5 cm)

c: 8 (8, 8½, 8½, 9, 9, 9½)"
(20.5 [20.5, 21.5, 21.5, 23, 23, 24] cm)

d: 3 (3½, 4½, 5, 6, 6½, 7½)"
(7.5 [9, 11.5, 12.5, 15, 16.5, 19] cm)

e: 10¼ (11, 11¼, 12, 12¼, 13, 13¼)"
(26 [28, 28.5, 30.5, 31, 33, 33.5] cm)

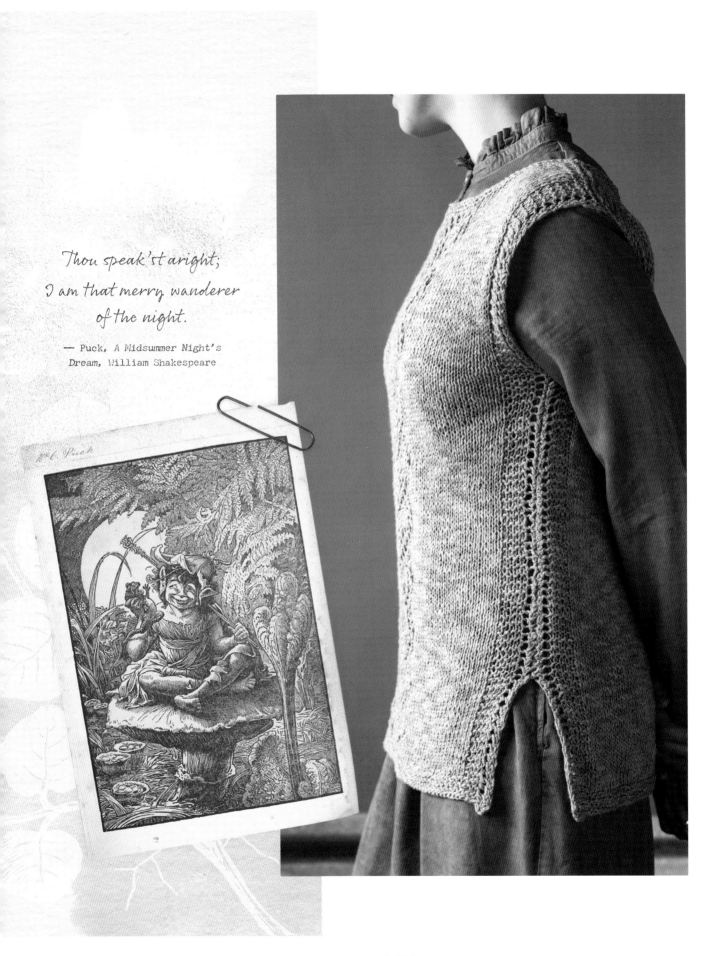

Thou speak'st aright;
I am that merry wanderer
of the night.

— Puck, A Midsummer Night's
Dream, William Shakespeare

taos tee

Taos, New Mexico, is known for many
things—art, chili peppers, culture, skiing, an
annual fiber festival, and more. The Taos Tee,
an airy layer featuring bands of lace diamonds
and a generous slit up the side, is inspired by all
those things. Wear it to a summer festival over a
linen dress, shorts, or your favorite flowing skirt.
This tee is worked from the top down in one
piece; for the best finishing results, take time
to block it to open up the lace pattern.

BY PAULA PEREIRA

finished sizes

Bust circumference: About 31½ (34¼, 38, 41¾, 45¼, 49¾, 53¼, 57)" (80 [87, 96.5, 106, 115, 126.5, 135, 145] cm).

Tee shown measures 34¼" (87 cm); modeled with 1¾" (4.5 cm) of positive ease.

yarn

Fingering weight (#1 super fine).

Shown here: Quince & Co. Sparrow (100% organic linen; 168 yd [154 m]/1¾ oz [50 g]): Maize, 6 (7, 8, 9, 10, 11, 12, 13) skeins.

needles

Sizes U.S. 3 (3.25 mm) and U.S. 4 (3.5 mm): 16" (40 cm) and 24" (60 cm) circular (cir) and set of double-pointed (dpn).

Adjust needle size as necessary to obtain the correct gauge.

notions

Stitch markers (m); stitch holders; tapestry needle.

gauge

22 sts and 30 rnds = 4" (10 cm) in St st on larger needle.

notes

— This tee is worked in the round from the top down with raglan shaping. Short-row shaping is used to raise the back neck. The sleeves are worked in the round from the top down.

— Slip stitches purlwise.

stitch guide

K2, P2 RIB IN RNDS (multiple of 4 sts)

Rnd 1: *P2, k2; rep from * to end.

Rep Rnd 1 for patt.

K2, P2 RIB IN ROWS (multiple of 4 sts + 2)

Row 1: (WS) K2, *p2, k2; rep from * to end.

Row 2: (RS) P2, *k2, p2; rep from * to end.

Rep Rows 1 and 2 for patt.

Yoke

With smaller, shorter cir needle, CO 108 (116, 116, 120, 124, 128, 132, 136) sts.

Place marker (pm) and join to work in the rnd.

Work in K2, P2 Rib (see Stitch Guide) for 7 rnds.

Change to larger needle and St st.

Inc rnd: K35 (37, 37, 38, 39, 40, 41, 42), M1, knit to end—109 (117, 117, 121, 125, 129, 133, 137) sts.

Shape back neck using short-rows as foll:

Short-row 1: (RS) Wrap next st, turn.

Short-row 2: (WS) Sl m, p39 (43, 43, 45, 47, 49, 51, 53), wrap next st, turn.

Short-row 3: Knit to m, sl m, work wrap tog with wrapped st, k3, wrap next st, turn.

Short-row 4: Purl to wrapped st, work wrap tog with wrapped st, p3, wrap next st, turn.

Short-row 5: Knit to wrapped st, work wrap tog with wrapped st, k5, wrap next st, turn.

Short-row 6: Purl to wrapped st, work wrap tog with wrapped st, p5, wrap next st, turn.

Short-row 7: Knit to wrapped st, work wrap tog with wrapped st, k7, wrap next st, turn.

Short-row 8: Purl to wrapped st, work wrap tog with wrapped st, p7, wrap next st, turn.

Short-row 9: Knit to wrapped st, work wrap tog with wrapped st, k9, wrap next st, turn.

Short-row 10: Purl to wrapped st, work wrap tog with wrapped st, p9, wrap next st, turn.

Short-row 11: Knit to wrapped st, work wrap tog with wrapped st, k3 (3, 3, 5, 5, 7, 7, 9), wrap next st, turn.

Short-row 12: Purl to wrapped st, work wrap tog with wrapped st, p3 (3, 3, 5, 5, 7, 7, 9), wrap next st, turn.

Short-row 13: Knit to m.

Next rnd: Working wraps tog with wrapped sts, k15 for left sleeve, pm for raglan, k40 (44, 44, 46, 48, 50, 52, 54) for front, pm for raglan, k15 for right sleeve, pm for raglan, k39 (43, 43, 45, 47, 49, 51, 53) for back.

Inc rnd: [K1, LLI, knit to 1 st before m, RLI, k1] 4 times—8 sts inc'd.

Next rnd: Knit.

Rep last 2 rnds 0 (1, 1, 1, 1, 1, 1, 1) more time(s)—117 (133, 133, 137, 141, 145, 149, 153) sts: 41 (47, 47, 49, 51, 53, 55, 57) sts for back, 42 (48, 48, 50, 52, 54, 56, 58) sts for front, 17 (19, 19, 19, 19, 19, 19, 19) sts for each sleeve.

Inc rnd: K1, LLI, knit to 1 st before m, RLI, k1, sl m, k1, LLI, k2 (5, 5, 6, 3, 4, 5, 6), pm for chart, work Front chart for your size over 37 (37, 37, 37, 45, 45, 45, 45) sts, pm for chart, [knit to 1 st before m, RLI, k1, sl m, k1, LLI] 2 times, knit to last st, RLI, k1—125 (141, 141, 145, 149, 153, 157, 161) sts: 43 (49, 49, 51, 53, 55, 57, 59) sts for back, 44 (50, 50, 52, 54, 56, 58, 60) sts for front, 19 (21, 21, 21, 21, 21, 21, 21) sts for each sleeve.

Next rnd: [Knit to m, sl m] 2 times, work chart to m, sl m, [knit to m, sl m] 3 times.

Inc rnd: [K1, LLI, work to 1 st before raglan m, RLI, k1] 4 times—8 sts inc'd.

Rep Inc rnd every other rnd 1 (4, 5, 5, 5, 5, 7, 7) more time(s), changing to longer cir needle when necessary—141 (181, 189, 193, 197, 201, 221, 225) sts: 47 (59, 61, 63, 65, 67, 73, 75) sts for back, 48 (60, 62, 64, 66, 68, 74, 76) sts for front, 23 (31, 33, 33, 33, 33, 37, 37) sts for each sleeve.

Work 1 rnd even.

Inc rnd: [K1, LLI, work to 1 st before raglan m, RLI, k1] 3 times, k1, LLI, k1 (7, 8, 9, 6, 7, 10, 11), pm for chart, work Back chart for your size over 42 (42, 42, 42, 50, 50, 50, 50) sts, pm for chart, knit to last st, RLI, k1—149 (189, 197, 201, 205, 209, 229, 233) sts: 49 (61, 63, 65, 67, 69, 75, 77) sts for back, 50 (62, 64, 66, 68, 70, 76, 78) sts for front, 25 (33, 35, 35, 35, 35, 39, 39) sts for each sleeve.

 **note:** *When each chart is complete, remove m for that chart and work those sts in St st.*

Next rnd: [Knit to m, sl m] 2 times, work Front chart to m, sl m, [knit to m, sl m] 3 times, work Back chart to m, sl m, knit to end.

Inc rnd: [K1, LLI, work to 1 st before raglan m, RLI, k1] 4 times—8 sts inc'd.

Rep Inc rnd every other rnd 15 (10, 11, 16, 17, 19, 21, 22) more times—277 (277, 293, 337, 349, 369, 405, 417) sts: 81 (83, 87, 99, 103, 109, 119, 123) sts for back, 82 (84, 88, 100, 104, 110, 120, 124) sts for front, 57 (55, 59, 69, 71, 75, 83, 85) sts for each sleeve.

Sizes 38 (41¾, 45¼, 49¾, 53¼, 57)" only
Work 1 rnd even.

Inc rnd: [Knit to m, sl m, k1, LLI, work to 1 st before raglan m, RLI, k1, sl m] 2 times—4 sts inc'd.

Rep Inc rnd every other rnd 2 (0, 3, 4, 4, 6) more times—305 (341, 365, 389, 425, 445) sts: 93 (101, 111, 119, 129, 137) sts for back, 94 (102, 112, 120, 130, 138) sts for front, 59 (69, 71, 75, 83, 85) sts for each sleeve.

All Sizes
Work 4 (12, 6, 1, 1, 1, 1) rnd(s) even.

DIVIDE FOR BODY & SLEEVES
Next rnd: Remove m, k1, place next 56 (54, 58, 68, 70, 74, 82, 84) sts on holder for sleeve, remove m, using the knitted method, CO 2 (5, 5, 6, 6, 8, 8, 9) sts, pm for new BOR, CO 2 (5, 5, 6, 6, 8, 8, 9) sts, k82 (84, 94, 102, 112, 120, 130, 138), remove m, k1, place next 56 (54, 58, 68, 70, 74, 82, 84) sts on holder for sleeve, remove m, CO 4 (10, 10, 12, 12, 16, 16, 18) sts, knit to end of rnd—173 (189, 209, 229, 249, 273, 293, 313) sts rem for body.

Body
Work even in St st until piece measures 8¾ (9½, 9¾, 10¼, 10½, 11, 11¼, 12¼)" (22 [24, 25, 26, 26.5, 28, 28.5, 31] cm) from underarm.

DIVIDE FOR SLITS
Next rnd: Remove BOR m, k6, place next 81 (89, 99, 109, 119, 131, 141, 151) sts on holder for front—92 (100, 110, 120, 130, 142, 152, 162) sts rem for back.

Beg working back and forth in rows.

Back
Next row: (WS) Purl to last 3 sts, sl 3 wyf (see Notes).

Next row: (RS) Knit to last 3 sts, sl 3 wyb.

Rep last 2 rows until slit measures 7¾ (8, 8¾, 8¼, 9, 9½, 9¼, 8¼)" (19.5 [20.5, 22, 21, 23, 24, 23.5, 21] cm), ending with a WS row.

Sizes 31½ (34¼, -, 41¾, -, -, 53¼, -)" only
Work 1 RS row.

back, sizes 31½", 34¼", 38", and 41¾"

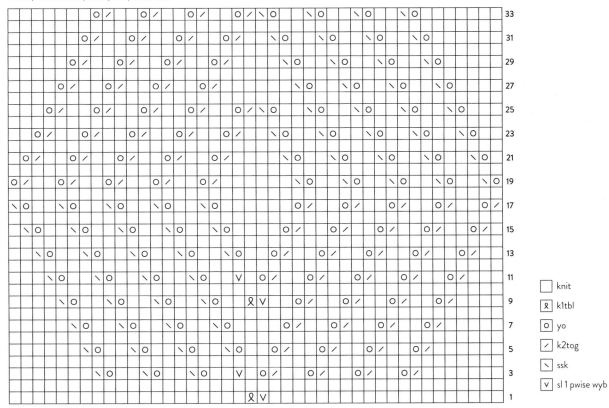

42 sts

back, sizes 45¼", 49¾", 53¼", and 57"

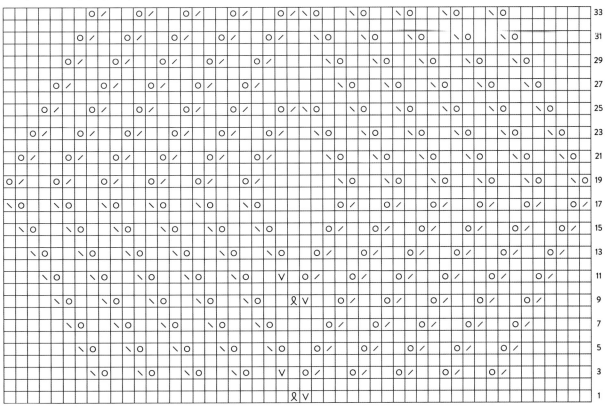

50 sts

front, sizes 31½", 34¼", 38", and 41¾"

37 sts

☐	knit
ያ	k1tbl
◯	yo
╱	k2tog
╲	ssk
∨	sl 1 pwise wyb

front, sizes 45¼", 49¾", 53¼", and 57"

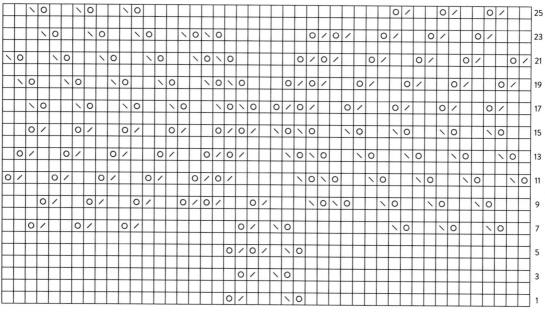

45 sts

Sizes - (-, 38, -, 45¼, 49¾, -, 57)" only
Next row: (RS) K3, ssk, knit to last 5 sts, k2tog, sl 3 wyb — – (108, -, 128, 140, -, 160) sts rem.

All Sizes
Change to smaller needle.

Next row: (WS) P3, work in K2, P2 Rib (see Stitch Guide) to last 3 sts, sl 3 wyf.

Next row: (RS) K3, work in rib to last 3 sts, sl 3 wyb.

Rep last 2 rows 10 more times.

BO all sts in patt.

Front

Return 81 (89, 99, 109, 119, 131, 141, 151) held front sts to needle.

With RS facing, pick up and knit 3 sts along top of 3 edge sts from back, knit to end, pick up and knit 3 sts along top of 3 edge sts from back—87 (95, 105, 115, 125, 137, 147, 157) sts total.

Next row: (WS) Purl to last 3 sts, sl 3 wyf.

Next row: (RS) Knit to last 3 sts, sl 3 wyb.

Rep last 2 rows until slit measures 7¾ (8, 8¾, 8¼, 9, 9½, 9¼, 8¼)" (19.5 [20.5, 22, 21, 23, 24, 23.5, 21] cm), ending with a WS row.

Sizes 31½ (34¼, -, 41¼, -, -, 53¼, -)" only
Inc row: (RS) Knit to last 3 sts, LLI, sl 3 wyb—88 (96, -, 116, -, -, 148, -) sts.

Sizes – (-, 38, -, 45¼, 49¾, -, 57)" only
Dec row: (RS) Knit to last 5 sts, k2tog, sl 3 wyb — – (-, 104, -, 124, 136, -, 156) sts rem.

All Sizes
Change to smaller needle.

Next row: (WS) P3, work in K2, P2 Rib to last 3 sts, sl 3 wyf.

Next row: (RS) K3, work in rib to last 3 sts, sl 3 wyb.

Rep last 2 rows 10 more times.

BO all sts in patt.

Sleeves

Place 56 (54, 58, 68, 70, 74, 82, 84) held sleeve sts onto larger dpn.

With RS facing, beg at center of underarm, pick up and knit 2 (5, 5, 6, 6, 8, 8, 9) sts along underarm CO, k56 (54, 58, 68, 70, 74, 82, 84) sleeve sts, pick up and knit 2 (5, 5, 6, 6, 8, 8, 9) sts along underarm CO—60 (64, 68, 80, 82, 90, 98, 102) sts total.

Pm and join in the rnd.

Work 2 rnds in St st.

Dec rnd: K1, k2tog, knit to last 3 sts, ssk, k1—2 sts dec'd.

Rep Dec rnd every 5 (8, 5, 5, 5, 4, 4, 4)th rnd 5 (3, 5, 7, 8, 12, 12, 14) more times—48 (56, 56, 64, 64, 64, 72, 72) sts rem.

Work 1 rnd even.

Work Rows 1–13 of Sleeve chart 2 times.

Work 4 rnds in St st.

Change to smaller dpn.

Work 7 rnds in K2, P2 Rib.

BO all sts in patt.

Finishing

Weave in ends. Block to measurements.

sleeve chart

knit
k1tbl
yo
k2tog
ssk
sl 1 pwise wyb
pattern repeat

8-st rep

Do you understand the stillness
Of this house
In Taos

— Langston Hughes, "A House in Taos"

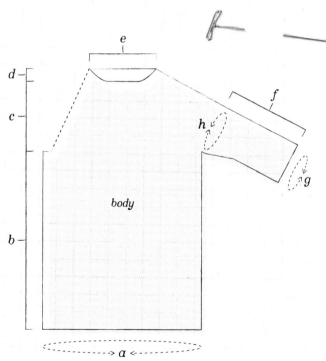

a: 31½ (34¼, 38, 41¾, 45¼, 49¾, 53¼, 57)"
(80 [87, 96.5, 106, 115, 126.5, 135, 145] cm)

b: 19 (20, 21, 21, 22, 23, 23, 23)"
(48.5 [51, 53.5, 53.5, 56, 58.5, 58.5, 58.5] cm)

c: 7 (7¾, 8¼, 8¼, 9½, 10¼, 11¼, 12)"
(18 [19.5, 21, 21, 24, 26, 28.5, 30.5] cm)

d: 1½" (3.8 cm)

e: 7 (7¾, 7¾, 8¼, 8½, 9, 9¼, 9¾)"
(18 [19.5, 19.5, 21, 21.5, 23, 23.5, 25] cm)

f: 9¾ (9¾, 9¾, 11¼, 11¾, 13, 13, 14)"
(25 [25, 25, 28.5, 30, 33, 33, 35.5] cm)

g: 8¾ (10¼, 10¼, 11¾, 11¾, 11¾, 13, 13)"
(22 [26, 26, 30, 30, 30, 33, 33] cm)

h: 11 (11¾, 12¼, 14½, 15, 16¼, 17¾, 18½)"
(28 [30, 31, 37, 38, 41.5, 45, 47] cm)

ARIZONA TEE

The Arizona Tee is an oversized, versatile, lightweight summer top you can layer over a tank and shorts, a sundress, or a swimsuit. Its straightforward construction lets you focus on the lacework; after blocking the pieces, seam them together and bask in the sun.

by amy gunderson

finished size
Bust circumference: About 41½ (48½, 55, 62, 68½)" (105.5 [123, 139.5, 157.5, 174] cm) bust circumference.

Tee shown measures 48½" (123 cm); modeled with 18½" (47 cm) of positive ease.

yarn
Lace weight (#0 lace).

Shown here: Fibra Natura Flax Lace (100% linen; 547 yd [500 m]/3½ oz [100 g]): #102 pale blush, 2 (2, 3, 3, 4) skeins.

Needles
Size U.S. 3 (3.25 mm): 16" (40 cm) circular (cir). Size U.S. 4 (3.5 mm): straight.

Adjust needle size as necessary to obtain the correct gauge.

notions
Marker (m); removable m; stitch holder; tapestry needle.

gauge
19 sts and 27 rows = 4" (10 cm) in lace patt on larger needles.

notes
—This tee is worked back and forth in separate pieces and seamed.

stitch guide

K1, P1 RIB (odd number of sts)

Row 1: (RS) *K1, p1; rep from * to last st, k1.

Row 2: (WS) *P1, k1; rep from * to last st, p1.

Rep Rows 1 and 2 for patt.

K1, P1 RIB (even number of sts)

Row 1: *K1, p1; rep from * to end.

Rep Row 1 for patt.

SLOPED BO

On last row before BO, sl last st pwise. BO row [sl 1 pwise] 2 times, pass 2nd st over first to BO 1 st, BO rem sts as usual.

Back

With larger needles, CO 99 (115, 131, 147, 163) sts. Work in K1, P1 Rib (see Stitch Guide) for 1½" (3.8 cm), ending with a WS row.

Work Rows 1–36 of Lace chart 5 (5, 5, 5, 6) times, then work Rows 1–6 (1–6, 1–20, 1–20, 1–6) once more; piece measures about 29 (29, 31¼, 31¼, 34½)" (73.5 [73.5, 79.5, 79.5, 87.5] cm) from CO.

BO all sts.

Front

Work as for back until piece measures 25 (25, 27¼, 27¼, 30½)" (63.5 [63.5, 69, 69, 77.5] cm) from CO, ending with a WS row.

SHAPE NECK
Next row: (RS) Work 39 (46, 54, 61, 69) sts and place these sts on holder for left front, BO 21 (23, 23, 25, 25) sts, work to end—39 (46, 54, 61, 69) sts rem for right front.

RIGHT FRONT
Work 1 WS row even. At beg of RS rows, using the sloped method (see Stitch Guide), BO 6 sts once, BO 3 sts once, then BO 2 sts once—28 (35, 43, 50, 58) sts rem.

Work 1 WS row.

Dec row: (RS) K2, k2tog, work to end—1 st dec'd.

Rep Dec row every RS row once more, then every 4th row once—25 (32, 40, 47, 55) sts rem.

Work even until piece measures about 29 (29, 31¼, 31¼, 34½)" (73.5 [73.5, 79.5, 79.5, 87.5] cm) from CO, ending with Row 6 (6, 20, 20, 6) of chart.

BO all sts.

LEFT FRONT
Return 39 (46, 54, 61, 69) held left front sts to needle and, with WS facing, rejoin yarn. At beg of WS rows, using the sloped method, BO 6 sts once, BO 3 sts once, then BO 2 sts once—28 (35, 43, 50, 58) sts rem.

Work 2 rows even.

Dec row: (RS) Work to last 4 sts, ssk, k2—1 st dec'd.

Rep dec row every RS row once more, then every 4th row once—25 (32, 40, 47, 55) sts rem.

Work even until piece measures about 29 (29, 31¼, 31¼, 34½)" (73.5 [73.5, 79.5, 79.5, 87.5] cm) from CO, ending with Row 6 (6, 20, 20, 6) of chart.

BO all sts.

lace chart

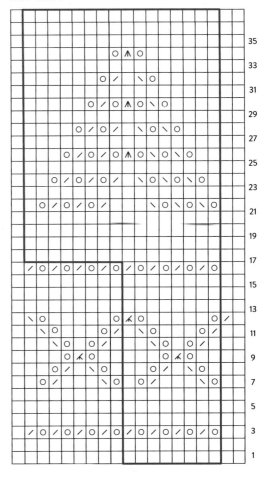

☐ k on RS; p on WS

• p on RS; k on WS

╱ k2tog on RS; p2tog on WS

╲ ssk on RS; ssp on WS

○ yo

⋌ k3tog on RS; p3tog on WS

⋏ cdd: sl2, k1, p2sso

☐ pattern repeat

a: 20¾ (24¼, 27½, 31, 34¼)"
(52.5 [61.5, 70, 78.5, 87] cm)

b: 21 (20½, 21¼, 21¾, 24½)"
(53.5 [52, 54, 55, 62] cm)

c: 8 (8½, 9, 9½, 10)"
(20.5 [21.5, 23, 24, 25.5] cm)

d: 5¼ (6¾, 8½, 10, 11½)"
(13.5 [17, 21.5, 25.5, 29] cm)

e: 10¼ (10¾, 10¾, 11¼, 11¼)"
(26 [27.5, 27.5, 28.5, 28.5] cm)

f: 4" (10 cm)

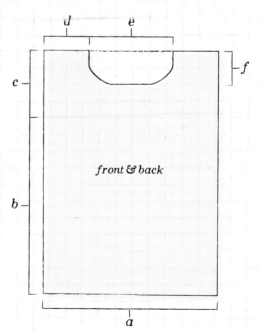

It's possible to enjoy wearing a knitted garment in the desert heat— just combine linen, lace, and a breathable gauge.

Finishing

Weave in ends. Block pieces to measurements.

Sew shoulder seams.

ARMHOLE EDGING

Place removable m on front and back 8 (8½, 9, 9½, 10)" (20.5 [21.5, 23, 24, 25.5] cm) from shoulder seam. With larger needles and RS facing, pick up and knit 80 (84, 90, 94, 100) sts between m.

Work in K1, P1 Rib (see Stitch Guide) for 7 rows.

BO all sts in patt.

Sew side seams, including armhole edging.

NECK EDGING

With smaller cir needle and RS facing, pick up and knit 49 (51, 51, 53, 53) sts along back neck edge, 25 sts along left front neck edge, 21 (23, 23, 25, 25) sts along front neck BO edge, 25 sts along right front neck edge—120 (124, 124, 128, 128) sts total.

Place marker and join in the rnd.

Work 7 rnds in K1, P1 Rib.

BO all sts in patt.

abbreviations

The following are the most common abbreviations that appear in this book. For other terms, be sure to check individual pattern stitch guides. For more advanced techniques or terms you don't know, please visit the Interweave online glossary: **interweave.com/interweave-knitting-glossary/**

beg(s) begin(s); beginning

BO bind off

CC contrast color

cdd central double decrease; slip 2 stitches at the same time kwise, k1, p2sso

cir circular

cm centimeter(s)

cn cable needle

CO cast on

cont continue(s); continuing

dec(s)('d) decrease(s); decreasing; decreased

dpn double-pointed needles

foll(s) follow(s); following

g gram(s)

inc(s)('d) increase(s); increasing; increase(d)

k knit

k1f&b knit into the front and back of the same stitch (increase)

k2tog knit two stitches together (decrease)

k3tog knit three stitches together (decrease)

kwise knitwise; as if to knit

LH left-hand

m marker

MC main color

mm millimeter(s)

M1 make one (increase)

M1L make one with left slant (increase)

M1P make one purlwise (increase)

M1R make one with right slant (increase)

oz ounce

p purl

p1f&b purl into the front and back of the same stitch (increase)

p2tog purl two stitches together (decrease)

patt(s) pattern(s)

pm place marker

psso pass slipped stitch over

p2sso pass two slipped stitches over

pwise purlwise; as if to purl

rem remain(s); remaining

rep repeat(s); repeating

Rev St st reverse stockinette stitch

RH right-hand

rm remove marker

rnd(s) round(s)

RS right side

sl slip

sm slide marker

ssk slip 2 stitches knitwise, then knit slipped stitches together

ssp slip 2 stitches knitwise, then return slipped stitches to left needle and purl 2 together through back loop

st(s) stitch(es)

St st stockinette stitch

tbl through back loop

tog together

w&t wrap and turn

WS wrong side

wyb with yarn in back

wyf with yarn in front

yd yard(s)

yo yarnover

* repeat starting point

** repeat all instructions between asterisks

( ) alternate measurements and/or instructions

[ ] work instructions as a group a specified number of times

TECHNIQUES

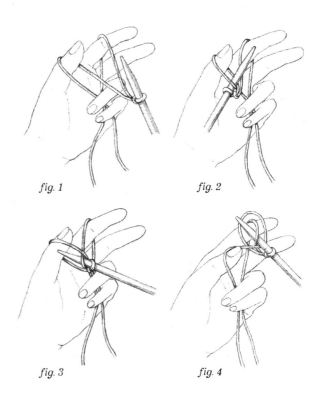

fig. 1   fig. 2

fig. 3   fig. 4

cast-ons

LONG-TAIL CAST-ON

Leaving a long tail (about 1–2" [2.5–5 cm] for each stitch to be cast on), make a slipknot and place on right needle. Place thumb and index finger of left hand between yarn ends so that working yarn is around index finger and tail end is around thumb. Secure ends with your other fingers and hold palm upwards, making a V of yarn (*fig. 1*). Bring needle up through loop on thumb (*fig. 2*), grab first strand around index finger with needle, and go back down through loop on thumb (*fig. 3*). Drop loop off thumb and, placing thumb back in V configuration, tighten resulting stitch on needle (*fig. 4*).

THREE-NEEDLE BIND-OFF

Place the stitches to be joined onto two separate needles and hold the needles parallel so that the right sides of knitting face together. Insert a third needle into the first stitch on each of two needles (*fig. 1*) and knit them together as one stitch (*fig. 2*), *knit the next stitch on each needle the same way, then use the left needle tip to lift the first stitch over the second and off the needle (*fig. 3*). Repeat from * until no stitches remain on first two needles. Cut yarn and pull tail through last stitch to secure.

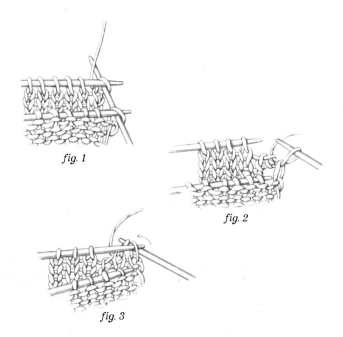

fig. 1

fig. 2

fig. 3

I-CORD BIND-OFF

With right side facing, cast on number of stitches needed for I-cord (as directed in pattern) onto left needle (*fig. 1*). *Knit to last I-cord stitch (e.g., if working a three-stitch I-cord as shown, knit two), knit two together through the back loops (*fig. 2*), and transfer all stitches from right needle to left needle (*fig. 3*). Repeat from * until required number of stitches have been bound off.

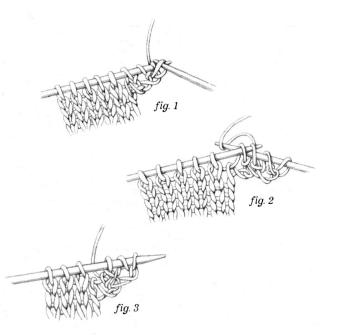

fig. 1

fig. 2

fig. 3

SUSPENDED BIND-OFF

This method is similar to the standard bind-off but produces a more elastic edge. Use it when you want to make sure your bind-off isn't too tight.

K2, *insert the left needle tip into the first stitch *(fig. 1)* and lift the first stitch over the second, leaving the first stitch on the left needle *(fig. 2)*. Knit the next stitch on the left needle *(fig. 3)*, then slip both stitches off the left needle—2 stitches remain on the right needle. Repeat from the * until no stitches remain on the left needle, then pass the first stitch on the right needle over the second stitch. Fasten off the last stitch.

Each bound-off stitch is slightly more elongated than with a standard bind-off *(fig. 4)*.

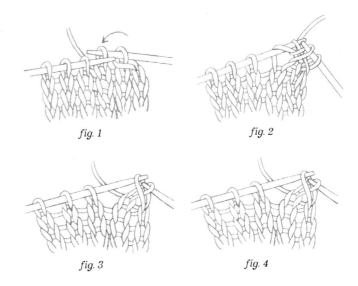

fig. 1   *fig. 2*

fig. 3   *fig. 4*

---

cables

RIGHT TWIST (RT)

Insert right needle into front of second stitch on needle and knit it, leaving stitches on left needle. Then knit first stitch on left needle, allowing both stitches to drop off needle.

LEFT TWIST (LT)

Insert right needle into back of second stitch on needle and knit it through the back loop, leaving stitches on left needle. Then knit first stitch on left needle, allowing both stitches to drop off needle.

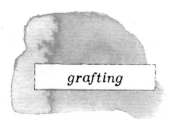

grafting

KITCHENER STITCH

Arrange stitches on two needles so that there is an equal number of stitches on each needle. Hold the needles parallel to each other with wrong sides of the knitting together. Allowing about ½" (1.3 cm) per stitch to be grafted, thread matching yarn on a tapestry needle. Work from right to left as follows:

Step 1. Bring tapestry needle through the first stitch on the front needle as if to purl and leave the stitch on the needle (*fig. 1*).

Step 2. Bring tapestry needle through the first stitch on the back needle as if to knit and leave that stitch on the needle (*fig. 2*).

Step 3. Bring tapestry needle through the first front stitch as if to knit and slip this stitch off the needle. Then bring tapestry needle through the next front stitch as if to purl and leave this stitch on the needle (*fig. 3*).

Step 4. Bring tapestry needle through the first back stitch as if to purl and slip this stitch off the needle. Then bring tapestry needle through the next back stitch as if to knit and leave this stitch on the needle (*fig. 4*).

Repeat Steps 3 and 4 until one stitch remains on each needle, adjusting the tension to match the rest of the knitting as you go. To finish, bring tapestry needle through the front stitch as if to knit and slip this stitch off the needle. Then bring tapestry needle through the back stitch as if to purl and slip this stitch off the needle.

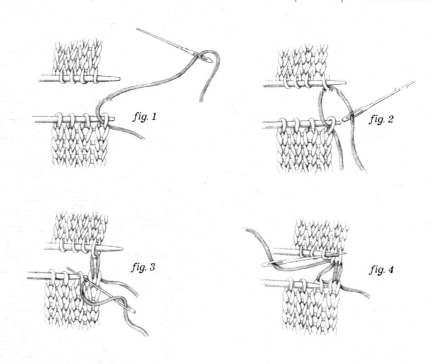

fig. 1

fig. 2

fig. 3

fig. 4

SINGLE CROCHET EDGING

Insert hook in stitch, yarn over and pull a loop through stitch (*fig. 1*), yarn over and draw through both loops on hook (*fig. 2*).

SLIP STITCH CROCHET EDGE

*Insert hook in stitch, yarn over and draw loop through stitch and loop on hook. Repeat from *.

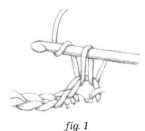

fig. 1

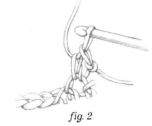

fig. 2

seaming

MATTRESS STITCH: VERTICAL TO VERTICAL SEAM

With RS of knitting facing, use threaded needle to pick up one bar between first two stitches on one piece, then corresponding bar plus the bar above it on other piece. *Pick up next two bars on first piece, then next two bars on other. Repeat from * to end of seam, finishing by picking up last bar (or pair of bars) at the top of first piece (*fig. 1*).

MATTRESS STITCH: VERTICAL TO HORIZONTAL SEAM

This method combines the mattress stitch method of picking up the bars between stitches on the vertical edge and working under stitches along the horizontal seam (*fig. 2*). Because stitches aren't square (they are wider than they are tall), you need to apply an easing to the seam. Typically, you need to work four bars (rows) for every three stitches.

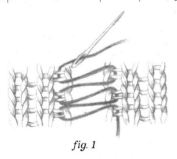

fig. 1

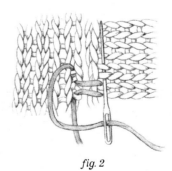

fig. 2

GERMAN SHORT-ROWS

With yarn in front, sl 1 pwise from left needle to right needle. Pull yarn to back of work over needle until both legs of stitch in row below are on top of needle (as shown), creating a "double stitch" on both sides of needle (*fig. 1*). When working the double-stitch on subsequent rows, work both legs together as a single stitch (*fig. 2*).

fig. 1

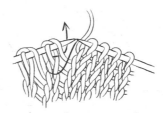

fig. 2

WRAP & TURN SHORT-ROWS

Knit Side

Work to turning point, slip next stitch purlwise (*fig. 1*), bring the yarn to the front, then slip the same stitch back to the left needle (*fig. 2*), turn the work around and bring the yarn to position for the next stitch—one stitch has been wrapped, and the yarn is correctly positioned to work the next stitch.

When you come to a wrapped stitch on a subsequent row, hide the wrap by working it together with the wrapped stitch as follows: Insert right needle tip under the wrap (from the front if wrapped stitch is a knit stitch; from the back if wrapped stitch is a purl stitch; (*fig. 3*)), then into the stitch on the needle, and work the stitch and its wrap together as a single stitch.

Purl Side

Work to the turning point, slip the next stitch purlwise to the right needle, bring the yarn to the back of the work (*fig. 1*), return the slipped stitch to the left needle, bring the yarn to the front between the needles (*fig. 2*), and turn the work so that the knit side is facing—one stitch has been wrapped, and the yarn is correctly positioned to knit the next stitch. To hide the wrap on a subsequent purl row, work to the wrapped stitch, use the tip of the right needle to pick up the wrap from the back, place it on the left needle (*fig. 3*), then purl it together with the wrapped stitch.

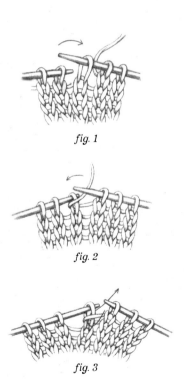

fig. 1

fig. 2

fig. 3

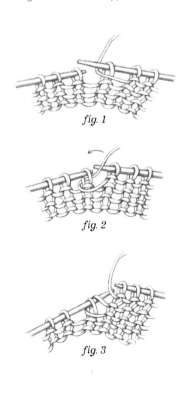

fig. 1

fig. 2

fig. 3

about the designers

MONE DRÄGER lives in a village in Germany and loves to craft and be creative. She can't imagine a day without knitting and enjoys playing around with colors and stitch patterns. Find her on Ravelry and social media as monemade.

AMY GUNDERSON lives in North Carolina with her husband and their two adopted dogs. If she's not knitting, it's only because she's busy dog cuddling.

Following an engineering career at Bell Labs and Jet Propulsion Laboratory, **MARGARET HOLZMANN** has returned full-time to her first love, knitting. She has been creating her own knitting designs since she was a teenager, but only within the last few years has she begun to consider herself a knitwear designer for others. She lives in Los Angeles with her husband and daughter and has three grown daughters.

SUSANNA IC has an extensive collection of studio arts and art history degrees as well as a rather large yarn stash. Her projects and designs can be found on Ravelry and at her website, artqualia.com.

JOANNA IGNATIUS lives on a small farm in southern Finland with her dogs. The nature around her, with Finland's changing seasons, provides endless inspiration for her designs. Knitting is a bit of a necessity for Joanna; like breathing, she really cannot live without it.

After leaving a career in architecture to be a full-time mom, **ILLITILLI** rediscovered knitting as a way to be both productive and creative in between nursing, naps, and diaper changes. She lives and knits on an island in the Salish Sea. Find her online atillitilli.com, and on Instagram as @illitilliknits.

ADRIENNE LARSEN is a designer and knitting instructor in Fargo, North Dakota. Her books *Welts & Waves* and *Flutter & Flow* are available now.

PETRA MACHOVÁ KOUŘILOVÁ inherited her passion for crafts from her mother, who taught her to knit when she was eight years old. Now a mama of two little boys herself, she spends most of her free time knitting, designing, and dyeing yarn. Her family home in the heart of Europe has been completely invaded by yarn.

Inspired by nature and whimsy, **MICHELE PELLETIER** is a vegan knitted accessories designer who loves bringing out the best in plant-based yarns. However, she can't claim that all of her knitted projects are 100% plant based; cat hair somehow manages to sneak into most of them. It's one of the joys of knitting in a home shared with kitties.

PAULA PEREIRA believes that inspiration comes from people, nature, and daily life and is played out using yarn and needles as tools. She is particularly fond of mathematics and geometry, which help her design garments and accessories. She lives in São Paulo with her husband, two dogs, and tons of beautiful fibers.

KIRSTEN SINGER-JOEL has been a knitter for the better part of her life, and a designer for the past six years. Her goal has always been to create patterns for the modern knitter—whether in lifestyle or fashion-style. She designs for knitters who want to relax at the end of the day with needles and fiber in hand and work on something that is purely for them. Kirsten designs for knitters who are always on the go and traveling but need to take their knitting with them.

NINA TALBOT was born and raised on a beautiful coast of the Russian Far East and now lives with her husband and three children in the equally beautiful Pacific Northwest. She has a degree in psychology and appreciates knitting for its therapeutic benefits. She hopes her designs will inspire more people to pick up needles and start creating. Find her knitting adventures on Instagram as @knit.share.love and Ravelry as nina-talbot.

ANNIKA ANDREA WOLKE is a UK-based knitwear designer hailing from Germany. She publishes knitting patterns under the label Annika Andrea Knits. She enjoys exploring textures and creating achievable knitting projects for all levels of knitting experience. When she is not knitting, she is an avid reader and often shares her book recommendations alongside her knitting endeavors on Instagram.

HOLLI YEOH's passion for knitting has spanned a lifetime, from learning to knit as a child to her fine-arts degree majoring in textiles and jewelry, and a fifteen-year designing career. A Holli Yeoh pattern is sure to offer something to learn, as well as a casually elegant aesthetic. Interesting techniques and clear instructions ensure a rewarding knit with beautiful results, as featured in leading publications and her book *Tempest*, published in collaboration with SweetGeorgia Yarns. See more of Holli's work and her teaching schedule at holliyeoh.com.

BOMBYX MORI

ABOUT THE AUTHOR

Cornelia Bartlette is a lifelong maker with current infatuations for fiber and shiny objects. Fastidious in some areas and downright reckless in others, her passion for making things with her hands is only matched by her love for her children and a well-attenuated stout. She resides in upstate New York and, yes, she has a cat.

mossy cyphel

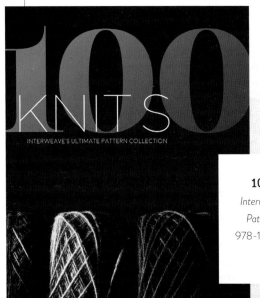
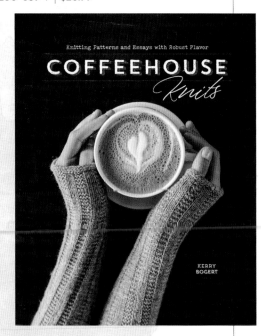